BONDAGE

BY CONSCIENCE...

LIBERATION

THROUGH
FORGIVENESS

BONDAGE

BY CONSCIENCE...

LIBERATION

THROUGH
FORGIVENESS
A MEMOIR

A STORY OF HOPE AND A BETTER TOMORROW

RAMONA LOPEZ

Foreword by Dr. Moses Mercedes

GET WRITE PUBLISHING

Bondage by Conscience...
Liberation Through Forgiveness
A Memoir
A story of Hope and a Better Tomorrow

Copyright © 2016 by Ramona Lopez

All Scripture references are from the New Living Translation Bible Version.

ISBN: 978-1-945456-38-1

Printed in the United States of America

Cover Design: Warrior Design Co.

Editor: Dr. Moses Mercedes

But whatever

I am now, it is all

because God poured out

His special favor on me

God who was working

through me by His grace.

- 1 Corinthians 15:10

CONTENTS

Dedication

Acknowledgements

Foreword I

Foreword II

Introduction

Chapter 1. **Blessed of God**   1

Chapter 2. **Major Loss**   7

Chapter 3. **Changed Life**   11

Chapter 4. **Saved to Serve**   17

Chapter 5. **Close Encounter: Divine Nature**   19

Chapter 6. **I Inherited the Property**   25

Chapter 7. **Journey into Deception**   31

Chapter 8. **Magnets**   35

Chapter 9. **It's a Question Mark**   43

Chapter 10. **Vanity**   47

Chapter 11. **The Dilemma**   55

Chapter 12. **Devastation**   61

Chapter 13. **Broken Relationships**   69

Chapter 14. **Slaves to Sins**   77

Chapter 15. **Defiance**   81

Chapter 16. **Victim**   85

Chapter 17. **Sovereign God**   89

Chapter 18. **The Past**   93

Chapter 19. **Unwise Decision**   97

Chapter 20. **The Pearls**   101

Chapter 21. **More Warning Signs**   105

Chapter 22. **What A Mess**   111

Chapter 23. **Can This Really Be Happening?**   117

Chapter 24. **Strange Occurrences**   125

Chapter 25. **The Critic**   135

Chapter 26. **Lost My Way**   141

Chapter 27. **Disobedience**   145

Chapter 28. **The Resurrection Hair Salon**   151

Chapter 29. **Two Thousand Seven**   155

Chapter 30. **I Lost It All**   159

Chapter 31. **Lord Help Me Keep My Sanity**   165

Chapter 32. **Mercy**   169

Chapter 33. **I Still Have A Purpose In Life**   173

Chapter 34. **Spiritual Awakening**   181

Chapter 35. **Hope**   187

Chapter 36. **Human Mistakes… Godly Responses**   191

Chapter 37. **I Am A Child Of God**   199

Addendum   201

Reference Page

DEDICATION

I dedicate this book to my beloved Harry, "the man who loved to drive." I had this quote engraved on his headstone because he was always driving me and the family somewhere. I enjoyed all of our road trips together.

I remember on one of those trips saying to him, when you died I'm going to write it as your epitaph on your headstone. It didn't dawn on me then what I was saying, that he would be dying before me.

I thank you Harry for imparting in my life the desire to go beyond my limitations and not just settle for less. He was my best friend. I thank him for taking me as his wife, even with all my imperfections (he knew them all.) I will be forever grateful to Harry. He was not a happenstance in my life. I'll see you in heaven my beloved.

ACKNOWLEDGMENTS

I am grateful to God and honor Him first and foremost for giving me the passion to write my story. Thank you Holy Spirit for guiding me through this journey. I thank God for shaping me into the woman that I am today. I use as my motto, I breathe and live Christ Jesus, my Savior.

I especially want to thank Dr. Moses Mercedes for taking time from his busy schedule to edit and proofread my book. I am honored and privilege to have had such a distinguish person as himself to help me in this endeavor.

I also like to thank Carole Myers for encouraging me to write my story. She was the first person I spoke to about the vision God had given me to write my story. I met her walking out of church one Sunday evening as I happen to glance over to my left and immediately was drawn to the shoes she was wearing. They were beautiful, their brilliant colors of aqua blue, green, silver, and magenta. I looked up and there she was this tall Caucasian elderly elegant-looking woman. I told her that her shoes were beautiful. She told me that she had painted them herself because she was an artist. I walked with her to the car and without much thought I asked her boldly how was it that she began to paint? Where did her desire to paint come from? She told me that the Holy Spirit inspired her to paint and she had been doing it ever since. She told me about some books she had about writing and asked me to come by her studio one day and so I did. She gave me a set of books that a former student had given to her, and the title of one of the books was, "If You Can Talk You Can Write," by Joel Saltzman. Hence, three years later I am publishing my own story and we are still friends. It was her enthusiasm for her own work that kept me writing when I wanted to stop.

I appreciate Bonita Robinson for inviting me to Prayer Tabernacle Church of Love where I met my spiritual mentor.

Thank you for your encouragement to take my writing talent to a new level.

I thank the Late Bishop Kenneth H. Moales Sr. for being my spiritual mentor and teaching me the powerful message of the gospel of Jesus and His Kingdom when I was a new convert in the church. I miss you dearly.

I also want to thank those who have in one way or another contributed to this endeavor either directly or indirectly through your prayers and your words of encouragement.

FOREWORD

From the lab of experiences, to the cry of a victim and the self-observation of change; Ramona goes through a learning process that has become a school of life to help others avoid the same mistakes and go to deliverance via the path of repentance, renewal, transformation, and forgiveness.

As she struggled with evil powers and her own demons of trauma and deception; to an encounter of illumination with her Savior and Lord.

I assure you, now reading this true story, that you will benefit from Ramona's experiences of intense thought patterns and emotions, to decisions for radical changes that free the Soul and heals the Mind; with a spirituality in harmony with the Word of God; and the Christian experience.

Intimacy dealt with transparency and honesty, detailed with a true picture of the human condition; of urges, wants, needs, passion, confusion; and the resources to confront all toward growing and maturity that brings deliverance and balance to life.

Knowing that Ramona's own therapeutic writing will be therapy to you the reader. I am please in writing this foreword.

Dr. Moses Mercedes

Master in Counseling
Spiritual and Family Adviser 35 years
Ordain Minister by the Assemblies of God
Apostolic Pastor 40 years
Radio Personality
Doctor of Divinity
E-mail: drmoisesmercedes@gmail.com

INTRODUCTION

A BURDEN TO TELL MY STORY

*"The blessings of the Lord make a person rich,
and he adds no sorrow with it."* Proverbs 10:22

This is a story about a time in my life when I chose sin over life. I refused to listen to God's warnings and did things that caused me to sin. This is a story of bondage by conscience and of liberation through forgiveness, especially mine. Through it all, I kept my faith. In my conscience I did not deserve mercy nor grace for what I had done, but for the grace of God. I believed that God is forgiving God but it was me who didn't want to forgive.

There was a heavy burden inside of me to tell this story about a period in my mid-adult life, that was full of lies and I foolishly subjected myself to it. I was deceived into thinking that the person I married only after meeting him six months earlier was the reincarnation of my late husband. I was a grown woman of fifty, and a godly one at that and my spiritual life was very important to me. I should have known better. To think that God would actually answer such a request. It was obvious that in my sorrow I had conjured up such a ridiculous idea. When I should've experienced joy and happiness in this new relationship, instead I became bitter and angry. I loathed myself for the person that I had become. I thought I was worthless. I became a prisoner of my own shame and guilt as a result of the ungodly things I did. The peace and joy that I entered this relationship with soon disappeared.

My heart became harden as the years past. Everything in my life changed. I was caught in a nightmare of my own doing and felt trapped in it. My every waking thought was about getting out of this nightmare, this marriage to a man I did not love. I'd ask myself the question over and over again, "What should I do?" I had the money to leave him and get my marriage annulled but I was confused and had lost all sense of direction. I felt stupid and dumb to say the least!

My conscience hounded me and it was a constant reminder of what a fool I had been. My guilt had gotten the best of me during those years of marriage to a man that I did not love I could not get rid of that horrible feeling of guilt. I blamed him for everything not realizing that it was me who should had been more vigilant so as not to fall prey to the flesh. I was in a dark place and was unable to see a way out. I thought that marriages like mine was only written as a script for a horror movie. I walked into a marriage arranged in hell and it became my worst nightmare! I had made the mistake of not thinking through the consequences of rushing into a relationship with a man that I had only met six months earlier. A man that I would end up loathing and despising. I would spend six years of our marriage living in guilt, shame, torment, fear, and confusion.

JOURNEY WITH ME

I invite you to take this journey with me as I share my experience with you about a time in my life when I widowed and remarried someone that I did not fully know. I have chosen to keep the names of people I write about out of the story and will only use the initials of two of the character's H and C. I wanted to believe that God had heard my prayers and give me back my beloved husband.

I did not take heed to the repeated advice and warnings from friends, family and even our pastors who expressed to us their concerns and they would say things like, don't you both think that you are rushing into this marriage. I rejected the voice of God that told me to run! Get away as far as you can! He is not for you! I left this marriage after six years and believed that I had forfeited any right to real happiness with another man. I was left financially unstable. I lost my properties. The worse part and most painful part about being in this marriage was the huge separation it created between my beloved children, their family and me. In my story you will experience my trials and tribulations that I had to go through because of my disobedience to God. But you will also experience his mercy and grace as he poured it out to me. I received the long awaited liberation from the torment of my past. As I share my testimony I hope that it would inspire you in some way.

CHAPTER 1

BLESSED OF GOD

"This is Solomon's song of songs, more wonderful than any other. Kiss me and kiss me again, for your love is sweeter than wine. How pleasing is your fragrance; your name is like the spreading fragrance of scented oils. No wonder all the young women love you! Take me with you; come, let's run! The king has brought me into his bedroom."

Song of Solomon 1:1-4 (NLT)

LIFE WAS SO GOOD

"Memories of his love and care will forever be imprinted in my mind and our relationship will remain one of a kind in my book. No pun intended."

I was widowed at the age of forty-nine during the summer of 2003. Before that period in time my life had been with such joy because I had a good husband, great children and adorable grandkids. I also had a lovely home in Stratford Ct where I had lived for twenty years. I hosted the picnics in my huge yard and the most elaborate parties. I would encourage my guest to dress up in their best garments because I enjoyed taking pictures. My home was always filled with the laughter of my children and grandchildren as well as friends, relatives and neighbors all having fun. I loved every minute of it.

There was so much peace in my home. For sixteen years after my conversion to Christianity my home had become a sanctuary where only the love of Christ was professed. My husband and I were both in love with the Savior and served in the church as an usher. I also volunteered in the Homeless outreach program on Saturdays. I helped with the cooking and serving of the dinners or organizing the community closet.

Life was good. I had a good job and we were both financially stable. We had a remarkable relationship that lasted until the very end, when he was called home to heaven. I loved him so much and I just couldn't get enough of him. We were always smooching. We just couldn't keep our hands off of each other.

MY BELOVED

My husband was also a very affectionate father and grandfather. Our grandchildren adored him. He was their grandpa. Whenever they came to visit, grandpa was always the center of attraction and they had plenty of hugs and kisses for him. I enjoyed having the family over for dinner. I'd cook their favorite foods. They especially liked my rice with pigeon peas and the roasted pork shoulder seasoned to perfection as the aroma of garlic, oregano, and cilantro filled the house. We'd all sit around the dining table and eat until we got full. Every time they came to visit I would have cake and ice cream, potato chips plus candies of all sorts as if it were someone's birthday. It made me happy to see their joy and hear their laughter.

I had a great relationship with my children and we would spend H a lot of time sharing each other's company. The relationship I had with H will never compare to any other. I was the happiest woman in the world... for the most part. I enjoyed his hardy laugh and I'd sit down next to him and watch comedy movies just to hear him laugh; I loved it was infectious. I was a proud wife because he was loved by many. I remember how his friends cried at the hospital and at his funeral.

I couldn't wish for a better husband because he offered me stability, a quality he'd learned from his father, (his father raised eight sons and was the sole provider). My husband made me feel safe and protected. I didn't have to worry about the monthly bills being paid or having the pantry stocked with food. I had only God to thank for that joy and happiness that I had experienced. God was blessing us in everything once we decided to seek Him as our personal Lord and Savior. He just continued to shower us with His love and mercy. God knew what he was doing when he gave me H as my husband. Memories of my husband's love and care will forever be etched in my mind and our relationship will remain one of a kind in my book. No pun intended. For twenty-four years, I was his woman and he was my man. He was the only man that I had ever truly loved. The only man who had ever made me feel good about myself. I felt such admiration for him. He'd compliment me every time I dressed up. When we'd go out on dates to a dinner or a movie, he would show how proud he was of me. He would tell me that he liked when other men admired me and they would do "double takes," then he'd say, you are mine and I get to take you home with me. H was 5'9 tall and I was 5'3. I considered myself an attractive woman and many of my friends compliment me on my pretty face and curvy figure and on my superb hostess skills. My food was always good and he'd boast about it to our friends and family. He encouraged me do better than I had done in the past. I don't deny that it was H who moved me out of the inner city/low-income neighborhood and took me to live in the suburbs. (Please I mean no disrespect to those of you who live in the inner cities.) I'm just making a comparison. Before his death, I had been accepted into the Master in Social Work program at Southern Connecticut State University (SCSU). I wanted to jump out of my skin when I was accepted into the program because it was considered the best Social Work program in the state. I looked forward to graduating from that school, since H had graduated from SCSU a few years earlier. I couldn't be happier!

REMARKABLE RELATIONSHIP

I had built so much confidence in him because he was my superhero and he took care of home. If something broke down he'd have someone fix-it. He was resourceful that way. I trusted him with my life because his 5'9" and 230 lb build was quite intimidating, although he was a teddy bear inside. I felt assured that no one was going to mess with me and our family. H was highly respected by everyone he came in contact with. He was truly my best friend. There was nothing he wouldn't do for me. One example of how much he loved me was how he replaced four sets of living room and bedroom furniture in less than twenty years only because I asked him to do it. I thought that was amazing and we were not wealthy; we worked for a living, so that was very impressive in my eyes. I must say it again that I was also blessed to have had a husband like H. He was such an exceptional guy.

From the very beginning of our relationship we had made a mutual covenant with each other to remain friends forever no matter what happened. I have to say that we did remain friends throughout our marriage until his death. Ours was a remarkable relationship that I will always value until the end. A relationship like the one I had with H will always remain one of a kind, there will be no other.

"I NEED YOU TO SURVIVE"

In December of 2002, I celebrated his fiftieth birthday with friends and family to show him my appreciation for everything he had done for me and the family. To see him happy was my goal and in turn, I was happy. His oldest brother rented the VFW (my brother in-law was a veteran) and there were at least 120 guests, mainly friends and family. The food was catered by one of the cooks from my job that had a private catering business. I asked my Pastor's oldest daughter to minister a worship dance for my husband. I chose the song by Hezekiah Walker, "I Need You To Survive." I stood next to him on stage holding his hand, as we looked into each other's eyes while she and four others from the church ministered that song. After the song, I hugged him and told him I love you and I can't survive without you. Little did I know that it would be his last birthday celebration.

OUR LAST VACATION TOGETHER

Our last vacation together was in May of 2003. We went on a cruise with my cousin, her husband and a couple that we had met up at the Catskills years earlier. We went swimming with the stingrays in the Cayman Island. We had plenty of fun on the ship, swimming, eating and dancing. He died two months after we came back; lost his battle with cancer. When he died I was so destroyed and hurt. I wanted to die. Yes, I wanted to just drop dead. I didn't want a terminal illness, I just wanted to die in my sleep. If someone had beaten me to a pulp it would not have hurt so much. Not having him by my side was torture. I thought that he and I would be together forever, until we both die in our sleep of old age; holding on to each other. That's how much I loved him. I really thought I would be a happy woman all the days of my life, but then the inevitable happened. I was very angry and could not understand why now, why me? I had it so good and I was living a decent respectable life. I as well as H had given up the drinking and drugging, which had been a part of our earlier lifestyle. I was then so truly happy with my new life. H and I had built a good thing together and so it seemed that the future looked even better than the latter for us both. So I thought.

CHAPTER 2

MAJOR LOSS

"He will wipe every tear from their eyes, and there will be no more death or sorrow or crying or pain. All these things are gone forever."

Revelation 21:4 (NLT)

GRIEF OVER MY LOSS

"Grief has a process that we must all go through in life when losing a loved one or something that is very meaningful to us."

I was torn apart when my beloved died. I felt alone in my grief and I cried for H every night and most days. Everything reminded me of him, my home, my street, the school, even the car. I eventually went to the dealer and traded in my 2003 Saturn Vue for a 2004 Saturn LS. My world had been radically changed forever; there was nothing that I could have done to reverse it. I wanted to wake up from the nightmare.

It was the month of October 2004 and I had just turned fifty years old, I had short blonde hair, my friends told me that I did not look a day over forty years old; and I still felt young and appeared younger than my stated age. I did not have any noticeable wrinkles on my face. My second oldest sister would ask me why don't you have wrinkles on your forehead? In my mind I wanted to tell her, because I'm not always pissed off like you are, but I would never tell her that. I took very good care of my face with Mary Kay products that I'd been using for over twenty-eight years. I considered myself attractive and I was in great shape. I was satisfied with my life and with what I had accomplished so far in that I had a good job and was about to start going to school for my Master's degree. I had received $50,000 from H life insurance policy. I was debt free, at the time of his death, and had plenty of money of my own in my saving and checking accounts. I was fortunate to have inherited one third of the property in Stratford that we both lived in for eighteen and a half years and one third of a three family house in Bridgeport. H and two of his younger brothers had a three-way partnership in these two properties.

ONE-YEAR ANNIVERSARY

On the one-year anniversary of his death in my desperate plea for comfort over my distress I knelt down in front of my bed, where I was accustomed to praying and told God, not asked Him, but told God, I am done suffering H's death and I want the strength to move forward. I am sick and tired of crying and suffering. But I did not wait for a response to my prayer.

Several weeks prior on July 21st of 2004, I had celebrated a memorial service for H with a few friends and family at his church with the priest who had married us presiding over the Mass. My duty in the service was to carry the holy water down the aisle and hand it to the priest and he mentioned H name and that made me feel like he was laid to rest and that my obligation ended there. After the service a few of our friends and family headed to the cemetery to pay our respect and admired the headstone that his oldest son had purchased which the epitaph read, (by my request) *"THE MAN WHO LOVED TO DRIVE."*

I had told myself that I didn't want to cry anymore over his death. It had been a painful year and I was just tired of the pain and suffering. It was then that I made the choice to move on with my life because I wanted to stop crying! I was angry that he was dead. That anger pushed me to a limit that I did not dare to go before and I told God angrily, I refuse to allow this world to tear me down anymore! I'm done crying! I have been crying and suffering since I was a child and I will have no more of it! No more! No more! When I got up from praying I made the decision to stop mourning H and move on with my life.

It wasn't that I wanted to put H's death behind me it's just that the pain was too great for me to bare and I thought that moving on was the best thing I could have done to save my sanity. I decided to stop grieving, not that I was going to forget my beloved, my longtime lover, companion, and friend. That was never my intent.

I realized later on through the years, that grief has a process that we must all go through in life when losing a loved one or something that is very precious to us. I had chosen to stop the process but the outcome of that decision wasn't what I had anticipated. I borrowed this quote by Molly Fumia, (she has authored several books on the grieving process) that was in Anne Roiphe's book, Epilogue: A Memoir (Anne wrote this book after she became widowed). Molly said, "that the grieving process is not something that a person can easily deny, stop, or challenge but that they must simply go through it."

I WAS ANGRY

I was so angry that H and I would no longer share intimate moments together and that I would never hear him laugh again. It would be that same anger that would drive me to journey in a direction not ordained by God. When I chose to give up on the grieving process, I also took my eyes off of God and began to focus on what I wanted; what I thought was best for me.

I thought that I was cemented in the word and that I was steadfast and unshakeable in my spiritual belief until H died and I began to doubt and question and lose all sense of direction. But really, I was a total mess and had no real guidance from anyone.

So I thought that I'd reinvent myself and that somehow it would essentially help me to survive this great loss.

CHAPTER 3

CHANGED LIFE

"When I was in deep trouble, I searched for the Lord. All night long I prayed, with hands lifted toward heaven, but my soul was not comforted."

Psalm 77:2 (NLT)

REINVENT MYSELF

"The course of my life would change dramatically, nothing would be the same. I would not be the woman I was before I widowed."

I started making decisions for the new me, the reinvented me, and I was going to conquer the world on my own. I pretended to know what was best for me and began to get myself involved in things I had no business getting into without the proper guidance. I made many foolish decisions along the way. The choices I made cost me greatly.

I regret it now, but I was determined to meet someone that would fill that emptiness that I was feeling in my heart, the need to be loved again. So one night, I went boldly to God on my knees, in front of my bed again and asked Him for a companion. I gave God details of how this man was to be. I told Him, I want someone who has his own business and own money, someone who attends church, and someone that would treat my family and me right. I also told God that this man had to have his own children because I couldn't have any more since I was going through menopause. I was very serious in my request to God. But, regrettably, I forgot several very important details that this person did not possess and that are essential in every marriage. I wish that I could've had a do-over but that only happens in the movies. As you continue to read

11

on and follow me on this journey it will be made plain to you how important friendship, honest communication and intimacy is in a lasting relationship.

I WAS FRAGILE AND VULNERABLE

I had not realized back when I was widowed what a fragile and vulnerable human I had become. I had forgotten who I was as a Christian. Then I began to question God and lost all sense of spiritual direction. I truly believed that I had strong biblical values and convictions that would keep me from wavering in my beliefs. I had been a believer, not just for several months but for over seventeen years. To lose sight of who I was in my faith was beyond my comprehension. I not only ignored that I was a child of God but I also lost sight of what really mattered to me, my beloved children and grandchildren. For as much as I love my family, I should have realized back then that it was just not a normal thing for me to do, I love my family dearly. That is when I should have noticed that something was not right with me emotionally, spiritually or mentally. It's not that I had given up on God, or stop believing in him, at least I didn't see it that way.

SELFISHNESS CREPT IN

In hindsight, I realized that I had become consumed with my own selfish desires and was unable to see the negative consequences of those desires that would later affect my life. The course of my life would change dramatically, nothing would be the same. I would not be the woman I was before I widowed. It would be further down the journey that I would realize that I had lost my dignity, my integrity, and my family. As you follow me down this journey into my new life you will see how my peace and joy were sapped out of me; and likewise how my kind and decent life all began to unravel.

I WAS PRETENDING

You see, I never lead on that I needed help and so everyone thought that I was doing alright and there was no need for my mental stability to be put into question. I knew how to pretend being strong, especially for the sake of my children and grandchildren. But a few of my friends found it very odd that I was getting married so soon. Several of my girlfriends questioned me about my decision to marry the new guy in my life and they asked, are you sure you want to marry this man who you just met and don't know anything about? One of my very dear friends told me right out, "I don't want to meet this guy and don't want anything to do with your wedding; you must be crazy!" I didn't think anything about it the, but I must had appeared like I was going through a period of temporary insanity. I saw her several years later in the park and introduced him to her, she was courteous but really didn't care to meet him. She and I were like sisters. We have not spoken to each other in years. I miss her, we were so close, I loved her dearly.

WHAT A MESS I CREATED

My marriage to a stranger would cause me to forfeit all that God blessed me with. I entered into that unholy matrimony and I chose a life filled with confusion, fear and hate as I began to loathe myself and my new marriage partner. I became a total mess, (The Merriam-Webster Dictionary describes mess as, "one that is disordered, untidy, offensive, or unpleasant usually because of blundering, laxity, or misconduct or a situation that is very complicated or difficult to deal with.") during that marriage I had no real guidance from anyone because I was ashamed to ask my close friends and family members for help.

MY MISTAKE

I made the mistake of rushing into something I was not prepared to handle. My plans were to start a new life where I would own a business and enjoy the wealth left to me by my late husband. Instead, I experienced something totally different that involved heartbreak and disappointment, one after another, all because I did not heed to the voice of God and began a relationship with a man that God had warned me against. I would loathe and despise this man the entire time that I was married to him and that attitude would hinder my relationship with God. I would spend the next six years of our marriage living in guilt, shame, torment, fear and confusion. Those years became my worst nightmare that I imagined I'd never wake up from.

I had no idea what I had gotten myself into until I was so deep down in the mud and was sinking deeper and deeper into oblivion. My thoughts did not give me rest as they constantly reminded me of what a "foolish woman" I had become. My thoughts became thorns in my flesh that tormented me day and night, saying things like, you gave up God to have sex with someone that you don't even love and he doesn't love you, you betrayed the memory of your late husband and you will not see him in heaven; your children and grandchildren are lost because of you, and on and on the insults would go. I began to feel the shame and the disgrace of what I had done. My guilt was compounded by my conviction as those things being revealed to me were true.

TOOK MY EYES OFF GOD

The truth was that I really did not love this man and that I had betrayed God for him. The truth was that I, in a moment of anger towards God, took my vision off of God. And, I was the matriarch of the family and should have been there for them. I really had not realized what my actions had done. Regrettably, looking back at what I had done, I tell myself if only I had waited a little while longer to see the plans that God had for me then maybe my life would had turned out much more rewarding and joyful, and less disgraceful and shameful. I had to endure being married to someone for six years that I did not love, that caused my guilt and shame to torment me day and night for those years of marriage. Then there were the constant thoughts of regrets that harassed me to the point of hating myself for making irrational and illogical decisions.

I ISOLATED MYSELF

The thoughts of what I had done to my family for marrying this man would cause me to isolate myself from them. I moved away from my beloved children and grandchildren because I was deceived into thinking that I had failed them. I was also running away from my own disappointments. I had put distance between my family and me. I, missed them so much I'd cry all the time until my head hurt, and that's how I fell asleep most nights. How did I come to be in such a state of mind? I was being held captive by my own conscious. Satan might ruin our plans and our lives but he will never ruin nor can he stop God's plans for our lives, and that's the truth! "But for the grace of God. I have been haunted for my mistakes for the past seven years. It was on the seventh year of my marriage that I started writing my story. I wish that I had never gone through those unexpected experiences that left so many unforgettable scars on me and my beloved family.

CHAPTER 4

SAVED TO SERVE

"The LORD did not set his heart on you and choose you because you were more numerous than other nations, for you were the smallest of all nations! Rather, it was simply that the LORD loves you, and he was keeping the oath he had sworn to your ancestors. That is why the LORD rescued you with such a strong hand from your slavery and from the oppressive hand of Pharaoh, king of Egypt."

Deuteronomy 7:7-8 (NLT)

SERVE IN THE KINGDOM OF GOD

Many years before the death of H, God had called me to ministry but I was not sure what kind of ministry. I knew that I liked evangelizing. I enjoyed sharing the word of God with people in my immediate circle, such as friends; neighbors, and my extended family. I remember being at a supermarket once and this female shopper tapped me on the shoulder and said, "You have the light of the whole world all around you." I knew deep down in me that I was "on fire for the Lord," and wanted others to know Him. No matter where I was, in a store, on the street, visiting friends and family I would talk about the love of Jesus Christ and His salvation with everyone. I wanted them to feel what I felt. I would encourage them to go to church.

I also wanted to sing praise and worship songs to my God in the choir and so I thought maybe I will be called to write music. I never did join the choir. I liked working with the homeless. I would help the church mother in the Homeless Outreach program or wherever she needed extra hands to pitch in. I was somewhat clueless as to what my true ministry would be. I had never mentioned to anyone, not even H that I wanted to have my own ministry someday. Do something big that would draw hundreds of people to God, especially the youth. I wanted to do more than just attend church on Sundays. I was just so anxious to do ministry and serve the Kingdom of God. God always knows what is best for us even when we don't have any clue.

CALLED TO THE NORTHEAST

I remember a time maybe three or four years before he died, when H and I had been discussing moving to Florida or maybe the Midwest, like Arizona. I prayed about it and the response I received from God came to me in a dream. God revealed to me that He needed me in the Northeast because that was where my ministry was to begin, right there in the church that I was attending. God was preparing me in that church, with one of the best Preachers and teachers that I had the opportunity to be under during my early years as a Christian. It was there that I was to start my training for my ministry.

The dream I had was about Jonah and God's request that he go to the city of Nineveh. Nineveh was in the far northeast part of the Assyrian Empire. Assyria is modern day Iraq. But instead, Jonah rebelled against God and made other plans that would take him to Joppa. Modern day Jaffa which is now surrounded by Tel Aviv in Israel in the far southwest. When I woke up that morning, I immediately took heed to what God had revealed and when I read the story in the book of Jonah, I put off moving out of Connecticut for several more years. But I continued to wait on the Lord for my calling. I never figured into the equation that I would be doing ministry without my husband.

CHAPTER 5

CLOSE ENCOUNTER: DIVINE NATURE

"God saved you by his grace when you believed. And you can't take credit for this; it is a gift from God." Ephesians 2:8 (NLT)

MY FIRST ENCOUNTER WITH A DEAR FRIEND

"God saved a wretch like me."

I became a Christian at an unusual time in my life. It all began with an unexpected encounter in the summer of 1987, when an old friend from my old neighborhood invited me to attend one of her church's Sunday services. This friend had been my neighbor for several years when we lived in the same apartment building, (I was on the first floor and she on the second) in the west end of the city of Bridgeport back in 1976. She was an African American about 5'9", on the heavy side, with a pretty face; who carried herself with such grace. Our families would come together for drinks, listen to music and have a wonderful quiet evening just talking, while the kids (my daughter and her son who were both four years old) played in the room. They moved away and we lost all contact with one another for over ten years. Then, on that peculiar day we ran into each other in the downtown area as we were crossing the street in the opposite direction. We were both so excited to see each other that we embrace for a long time. We talked about how we were both doing and what we were doing at the present time. Then she invited me to her church.

I felt so uncomfortable with the invitation that I wished she had not mentioned church. I did not know her back then (1975) as a Christian and so I realized then in our encounter that she was serious about it and wanted to share it with me but I was not ready, so I thought. Her church was located on the eastside of the city, and I knew the area very well, since I had lived only a few blocks from the church some years before. That church had been an old Greek Orthodox Church back in the sixties and seventies. It still had the gold dome on the roof top, with its faded blue and white trimmings around the wooded window and door frames, with the red brick walls that surrounded the building holding it together for all those years. Because of the neighborhood's bad reputation for drugs and gangs a fence of black wrought iron had to be built around it to keep it from being vandalized. After that first encounter, I kept running into my friend at the same area and I'm not quite sure what I was doing there.

I would always make up some excuse as to why I could not stop and talk to her much. In hindsight, I felt bad about lying to her and walking away, leaving her with the words in her mouth. For example, she would be talking to me and before she could finish her sentence I would be waving goodbye from a distance. You see now I know that God was calling me. God had a plan and no matter how hard I tried to get away from Him, He would put my dear friend before me to encourage me. I kept running into her in the strangest places and she would always ask me to come to her church and again I would run from her. I'm not sure how long these encounters went on but after much resistance, I finally decided to go to her church and it was at her church that I had my first experience with the Holy Spirit and it was there where I received Jesus Christ as my Lord and Savior.

MY ENCOUNTER WITH THE HOLY SPIRIT

One Sunday the Pastor had asked members to come up to the pulpit and stand in the presence of the Holy Spirit. I decided to go because I wanted to be bathed in His presence. As I'm standing there praising God with my eyes closed, I felt myself going down as if in slow-motion, I ended up on the floor lying face-up.

As I am lying on the floor my right and left arms began to stretch out slowly at the same time, I crossed my legs at the ankle and I'm just lying there. Then the strangest thing happens I feel a piercing sensation going through the palms of both hands and I moan faintly as if in pain but I'm not hurting and again the piercing sensation but this time it's on both my feet and I moan again; after a while I get another piercing sensation going through the lower part of my hip and I moan again ever so faintly. I still can't open my eyes, I can't even move and I'm not sure what is taking place except that this was how Jesus was crucified. The next thing that happens is my arms start moving straight up to the ceiling, I'm still down on the floor and I can't open my eyes as if they were glued shut but I see a very bright light above me and I say these words, "God help me." I'm not sure if anyone is hearing me because I said it loud in my mind because I couldn't verbalize words when I was on the floor all that time but then another voice whispers "It is finished." Eventually, I was able to open my eyes and was assisted up from the floor. I went back to my seat, the Pastor said a closing prayer and dismissed the members. I would become an advent church-goer.

Every Sunday, I would spend hours in church praising and worshipping my God and would love every minute of it. I was on fire for this Jesus who had saved me time and time again from the grips of the devil even when I did not know Him. Jesus also saved me from my destructive self and from dying in my sin. God who loved (still loves me) me even when I was doing drugs (almost died of an overdose), and who would bring me safely home even when I couldn't remember how I got there because I had gotten so drunk the night before while hanging out in the after-hours. "God saved a wretch like me." Some years into my new found faith, I knew that God had saved my life so that I would do ministry but I was not sure what kind.

GOD-FEARING PEOPLE

Both H and I became God fearing people and we both attended our own selective churches, he went to the Roman Catholic Church on the east side of Bridgeport, specifically the one he had attended as a child with his parents. It was the same one where we got married. Well, it wasn't exactly the same one because they tore down the old building and built a new one in the same location. I went to the Assembly of God in Christ church on the east end of the same city. We both had good jobs, he was the second shift manager of a candy manufacturing plant in Milford, CT. I worked doing case-management for a state agency in Bridgeport. We were living life to the fullest and life was so wonderful, God made it so.

ENCOUNTER WITH DEATH, MY BELOVED HUSBAND

His death was very devastating to me, to say the least, and for our children as well. When this happened, I got angry at God and blamed Him for taking my husband to heaven with Him. I argued with God to give him back to me but I knew that it wasn't realistic what I was asking. How dare I have an attitude with God! I had a long conversation with God and told Him what I was going to do with my life. "Imagine that!" Me telling God what I was going to do with my life, as if my life belonged to me. My life was bought with a price at Calvary and Jesus Christ my Savior was beaten, bled and took the pain for me. I was full of myself at that time and I had no idea where it was coming from. I blamed God from that moment on because he had taken my husband to heaven with Him. I never thought for one moment that I would open the portals of hell and open myself up to become Satan's next victim. God had plans for my life and Satan's schemes were to upset those plans. God's chosen children for the most part, will seek His kingdom and seek to draw others to the faith.

"Stay alert! Watch out for your great enemy, the devil. He prowls around like a roaring lion, looking for someone to devour." 1 Peter 5:8 (NLT)

Satan most certainly watches and waits to see. When I decided to ignore God's warnings, the inevitable happened which brought negative consequences to my life. This soon began to ripple down into the lives of my family.

CHAPTER 6

I INHERITED
THE PROPERTY

"For the love of money is the root of all kinds of evil. And some people, craving money, have wandered from the true faith and pierced themselves with many sorrows." 1 Timothy 6:10 (NLT)

I'M STARTING A BUSINESS

"My New Business Venture..."

I had been working a lot of overtime in the inpatient units at the Greater Bridgeport Community Mental Health Center for the past two years. I was thinking about using that extra cash as well as the rest of the insurance money to invest in a business venture. I thought about opening up a Christian book store or a hair salon/barber shop. I had intentions of using the business as a means to share the love and word of God with the customers. I also wanted to know what it felt like to be a businesswoman and have something that I could call my own. I set out to look for people that I knew and trusted who would know someone that they trusted, a relative preferably, who was willing to help me.

It was towards the beginning of August in the summer of 2004 that I put that idea into motion. I was working overtime on the sixth floor and it was my turn to watch a patient. At the same time, my friend, who I had befriended two years earlier, also had a patient to watch. We happened to have the same assigned room and were sitting across from each other. The patients were asleep and I began to tell her about my new business venture. I said, I want to open a book store or maybe a hair salon but before I do anything I first have to get someone to fix the leak coming from the ceiling. I told her, that I owned one third of the property of a multi-family house that I inherited from my late husband. I shared that my brother in-law was allowing me to take the store and the first floor apartment. This apartment had been unlivable for some time and both the store and the apartment needed plenty of fixing. The roof over the shop had been leaking and it ruined the ceiling inside the store.

She told me about her nephew C and mentioned that he was a roofer and she would tell him about my needing help with repairs. I'll give you his cell phone number and you call him, she said. I'll call him immediately and set a time for tomorrow after work, I told her. I was so excited to get my business up and running and just couldn't wait to meet him.

IT WAS A MEAT MARKET

The property where the house/shop was located happened to be on a busy avenue on the west end of Bridgeport. There were many other businesses and privately owned multi-family houses around. The area was for the most part well-kept by most of the property owners. My property had been previously owned by a Polish family and the store had been a meat market. When my late husband and his brothers bought the property, H opened a liquor store and used the walk-in meat freezers for cold beer storage. I thought that a hair salon would be beneficial both to the neighborhood and me.

SHOULD I OPEN A HAIR SALON OR BOOKSTORE?

I remember that H and I had opened a hair salon back in 1993. My late husband invested the money to give our daughter her very own hair salon since she had graduated with her Cosmetology Diploma from Bullard Haven Technical School. We both thought it was a good idea at the time to give her a business of her own. He had the extra cash so why not.

However, it didn't work out quite the way we had anticipated and so we sold everything in the shop to someone who was opening up their own salon and it worked out for everyone.

I was debating and thought maybe opening up a book store/coffee shop would not be so bad. But I was wary about it at first and thought who would visit the store and read faith-based books, buy the books; and have coffee. Most customers from outside the area knew that this area wasn't the best area in town. Everyone knew about the low-income housing located around the corner from there. I thought that with all the drive by shootings, drug dealings and gang fights no one from outside the area would come. Although in my heart I thought that it would be a good idea to bring some better culture to that part of town. I would be giving back to the community and helping to improve the neighborhood. I thought why not have the low-income housing residents visit the coffee shop? Since my first intentions for opening up was to minister to everyone that needed a Savior, I shouldn't stereotype. I also came from the hood and lived in low-income housing in this same area for several years some thirty plus years prior.

PROPERTY NEEDS REPAIRS

I trusted my friend's recommendation to call her nephew and I had no reason not to trust her. I considered her a godly woman. I would see her on occasions sharing the scriptures with several colleagues and clients at the agency. She told me, "My nephew is a good man and he goes to church, and I highly recommend him for the job. He is also single," she added.

I was so anxious to get started on my new venture that I did not hesitate to call him the following day. He agreed to meet me at the property that same day after work. When he got out of the truck my eyes were quickly drawn to the vehicle that he was driving, it was a gold metallic Ford pickup that appeared new. I was impressed with the color of the truck and I don't know why that was important to me right then. I saw this stranger walking toward me. I asked him if he was C and he said, yes! I immediately felt the urge to trust him because his aunt C had told me he was a good man and I took it as that he was a godly man, (weird I know.) I pretended to be business savvy yet I allowed his actions to lead me into trusting him. How gullible I was. I showed him where the leak looked like it came from. There was a huge rusty looking circle of water stain on the ceiling panels. He went up to the roof to inspect it and when he came down, he said, "I'll repair it." I asked him, how much would it cost but he did not want to discuss payment at that moment and said, "I'll be back tomorrow and then we'll talk."

MEETING THE REPAIRMAN AT HOME DEPOT

I met him the following day after work, at around four thirty. When we met at the site, he had already made the repairs on the roof earlier that day. I asked him, "So how much do I owe you?" He said, "You don't owe me anything the guy upstairs will take care of it." I asked him, "What guy upstairs?" I was thinking maybe one of the tenants who lived upstairs from the business had paid him for the job. I insisted on paying him for the work but he continued to refuse payment and pointed to the sky. I said in a naïve way, you mean the God in heaven, and he said, yes! God will not allow me to charge you, and so I left it at that.

At that moment I thought, I need other repairs at the shop, why not ask him for the help. I thought to myself, he is a contractor and who better than him to get me some reliable contractors that would work for what I could afford at the time. I felt that I could trust him to find them for me. So, that was one less thing I had to worry about. He told me about this one guy that had done some work for him and that he highly recommended him. He added, that he is undocumented but he is good at what he does. I did not mind as long as the work got done, who am I to judge. One week later, I met with the guy and told him how much I was willing to pay for the entire job.

The shop needed all brand new wall panels, an entire new ceiling, up to code electric rewiring, new light fixtures, and a new toilet and sink. It also needed a brand new wood floor to meet the standards required by the city ordinances and standard building codes and new front windows. The contractor took the job and I gave him one fourth of the payment to get the work started. Later, C told me, he needed that money to take care of his family needs. I looked at all this as a blessing from God and felt that everyone was going to be blessed with this new venture of mine.

Because I was working so much overtime I couldn't take time out to go by the shop as often as I would've liked to buy the materials and supervise the work so I had decided to ask C if he didn't mind being the go between me and the contractor. I would meet C at the Home Depot store and purchase the materials needed for the repairs and then he would deliver them. I was so relieved that C had agreed to help me. We began to meet at Home Depot two to three times a week.

I CAN'T MANAGE PROPERTY ALONE

About three weeks after meeting C, I had the nerve to ask him if he didn't mind supervising the work being done at the shop. I told him, I work fulltime and I'm not available during the day and I thought since you are on the road most of the time you may be able to stop by and see if the work is getting done. He didn't hesitate to say yes to my request and I was relieved of that burden. C's job required that he travel around the neighboring towns doing job estimates, collecting money from customers, and buying materials for his own workers. I figured that he wouldn't mind stopping in every now and then to check with the workers just in case they needed more materials.

I had no idea of how clueless and ignorant I was for trusting people. I knew nothing about owning property and business and most of all handling big amounts of money. I know now that my pride played a part in my failure and for that I humbly regret it all.

I really thought that C was a blessing in disguise. I was so happy that he was helping me with the business and I couldn't be more appreciative of his help. My appreciation to him would cost me greatly in the end.

CHAPTER 7

THE JOURNEY INTO DECEPTION

"Don't be misled—you cannot mock the justice of God. You will always harvest what you plant. Those who live only to satisfy their own sinful nature will harvest decay and death from that sinful nature. But those who live to please the Spirit will harvest everlasting life from the Spirit."

Galatians 6:7-8 (NLT)

MY MIND DECEIVED ME

"I began my journey into a sea of deception and lies."

One night, in the beginning of September, I believe it was a Thursday, I was leaving the shop and something strange happened. I had just finished inspecting the work that had already been done in the shop, which was quite a lot. As I'm getting ready to turn the ignition in my car, I see C, whose truck is parked in front of my car, walking toward his truck but suddenly stops midway, turns around and starts toward me with a puzzled look in face. I roll down my car window he leans in and invites me out for dinner that Saturday.

I think about it for a while, I don't really want to go out with him, but I find myself thinking, well I am single and I'm not doing anything why don't I just go out with him it's only for dinner, and so I accepted. Then he paused and said to me, better yet I think I will cook dinner for you at my home. I'll make fried green plantains with marinated shrimp. This is a cultural Puerto Rican dish made with cooked mashed green plantains, with plenty of olive oil and minced garlic, and the shrimp is made in a tomato sauce with green peppers and onions to pour over the plantains.

This was a shocker to me. What shocked me wasn't the invitation to dinner or what he was going to cook for me. Let me explain why I thought it was such a shocker. I had never told C what my favorite foods were and that happened to be my very favorite dish. I could eat it every day. I was impressed that he was going to cook my favorite food so I said to him, yes I'd be happy to come to your home for dinner.

The shocker was that I started to entertain a weird thought in my mind. I thought that maybe God had heard my prayers about giving me back H and had answered it at that moment in time. I sat in my car wondering what was going on and how would C know what to cook for me since the only one who knew about my favorite food was my late husband H. I felt that it was the strangest thing and I could not get over thinking that only H knew this about me.

I BELIEVED IN THE REINCARNATION OF H

Every night for one entire year I cried uncontrollably over missing H and I'd ask God to give me back my husband. That night I believed the unimaginable happened, that God had answered my long awaited prayers and sent the spirit of my beloved H into the body of C. That was the most ridiculous thing ever but what was more ridiculous was that I believed it. I believed it in my heart. I was so delighted that I set in my mind to get to know C more closely and personally because God had granted my prayer request. I told myself that I would learn to love C. But in reality it wasn't C who I would love but the memory of my beloved H in the person of C and so it was then that I gave into the flesh.

I BELIEVED THE LIES

In hindsight, it was there and then that I began my journey into a sea of deception and lies. How foolish had I been to think such a ludicrous thing as that. I had no idea of what I had done. I was clueless and ignorant of how I allowed my thoughts to deceive me. The decisions I made then would forever change the course of my life. I flirted with sin and fell prey to the flesh. It was this kind of thinking that gave Satan a foothold into my life. He then set his plan in motion to create confusion, chaos and distractions in my life. Yes! Distractions! I would be clueless about what I had done. As far as I was concerned life went on as usual.

I went to C's apartment on that Saturday around 6:30 pm. His apartment was small and cozy. The front door to the apartment was in the small living room area which was overcrowded by an oversized dark grey fabric sofa and chaise to the right. Straight ahead in the corner was a computer desk, a tall 5-drawer filing cabinet, and the television was kiddie-corner, hanging over the computer desk. The kitchen was to the left of the living room and had a huge wooded table with four chairs and the bathroom, which was uncomfortably small, was next to the bedroom. I watched him prepare the remainder of the meal as we made small talk about the shop, nothing specific. His youngest daughter nine years old at the time, was visiting. She was so cute and I liked squeezing her hands, they were fatty like a teddy bear's paw.

We all sat down to eat dinner at the kitchen table. It tasted alright but it was not quite what I had expected. I asked him, "Where is the shrimp and the sauce?" he said, "I do mine this way, the shrimp is mixed in with the plantains." During the dinner, I was still thinking that somewhere in C was the spirit of H and that made things alright. I had a good night just talking and watching television, don't remember what we were watching and I went home after several hours.

THE DECEPTION CONTINUES...

After that night, he continued to invite me out and then we began to share some real personal stories and stuff about each other's past. He told me, on one of those dinner dates, that he played in a Pool League.

I asked, "How good were you?" He said, I played fairly well, winning most of the games for the team." That conversation brought back memories of when H played for a neighborhood bar and grill in Bridgeport. He was an exceptional pool player. Most of the bars in Bridgeport wanted H on their pool team. Many pool players sought him out because he was that good. They wanted to see if they could beat him. But they couldn't. I was really psyched that H's spirit was occupying C's body. I truly believed that God had given me favor and was showing me a glimpse of his supernatural powers. I began to be fond of him, not really falling in love with him but a need to be with him, maybe to be closer to H. I had not realized just how vulnerable I was during that time in my life.

I remember a Wednesday night Bible study at his church when the Pastor was teaching a lesson on how God will allow for those that serve Him to be attacked by the enemy, Satan, to see if they'd run from Satan and seek God's safety or stay and try to overpower Satan by their own strength.

Sometimes, Christians think that everything that seems right to them has to be from God but that is why Christians must learn to discern right from wrong. I definitely was not in the right mental or emotional state of mind to be able to discern if what was taking place in my life was from God or from Satan.

CHAPTER 8

MAGNETS

"Always be humble and gentle. Be patient with each other, making allowance for each other's faults because of your love. Make every effort to keep yourselves united in the Spirit, binding yourselves together with peace." Ephesians 4:2-3 (NLT)

THE HOUSE WHERE WE MET

I have realized one thing with this loss, that is being a Christian and following God does not prevent one from dying but the most important thing that we must learn is to depend on God and know that He will be with us forever throughout our trials and tribulations until we see Him face to face in Paradise, and that is what is important to remember. "We are only passing through this world for this is not our home. Our real home is in heaven, and that is where my beloved husband His."

It was the summer of 1978 and I had been invited by H's brothers to cook lunch for them and their friends while they painted the outside of the house. My two-year old son wanted to paint the house also. He painted over the freshly painted blue wall with white paint and they were not very happy. We got along really well. I had been friends with H's brothers for about four months before through a mutual friend. It was at H's home where I first met him. He and his brothers had purchased the house several years before for their elderly parents to live in but his mother lost her battle with cancer and his dad moved.

The house was located in a quiet residential neighbor-hood in Stratford, Connecticut. The upstairs was being rented out to a single mother and two kids. It was the biggest house on that block and it had the biggest lot (per square yards) with a silver medal frame fence built around it.

It had been a hot summer and I was inside the house where the air conditioner was blasting. I'm standing in front of the kitchen sink rinsing off the lettuce and tomatoes when I suddenly felt a presence behind me like someone watching me and when I turned around I caught H looking at me with this cute smile on his face. I have to admit that I instantly found him very attractive and was immediately drawn to him like a magnet is drawn to metal.

DRAWN TO EACH OTHER LIKE A MAGNET

That magnetic feeling between us would end up being our attraction trademark throughout our relationship. It was as if we had this invisible connection that pulled on us to connect. It was unexplainable. But whenever we were next to each other we could not control the urge to be in each other's arms smooching. Our relationship was a strange one to say the least and the feelings were so very strong for one another that we could not get enough of each other.

Well anyway, he had just come out of the shower and he was wearing a white t-shirt and blue jeans. He looked about six feet tall (he was actually 5'9), good built of nothing but muscle and he was very much a "hunk of a man" (in my estimation). My goodness, he was so handsome and deliciously cute, built like a solid rock he was. He wore a crew cut haircut and was so clean shaven. He wore a nicely trimmed black mustache over perfectly shaped lips, He had high cheekbones (some freckles around his cheeks), and a cute slim nose.

H looked great in his Caribbean, Latino deep tan. He was Puerto Rican, born and raised in Bridgeport CT but he was very island-looking. Of course, it was summer and it appeared that he had been in the sun for some time. He eventually introduced himself to me as one of the brothers. I was there at the house way into the night. We all ate and drank and had a great time that day.

HE DRIVES ME HOME

It was getting late and I had to get home with my two kids and I needed someone to drive me back home, since one of his brother had picked me up at my home earlier that day. He immediately volunteered to drive me home and I was more than happy when he had offered. It was obvious to the both of us that we wanted to spend a little more time with each other that day.

As he drove me home, we talked about his line of work. He had been a Correction Officer for the North End Correctional Department in Bridgeport CT several months before we met. I shared what I wanted to accomplish in life. Since I still had two small children to care for and they needed my full attention so I had to put my life on hold.

He was working as the night manager at a neighborhood bar and grill that was owned by his best friend. Neither one of us wanted to start a serious relationship with anyone because we both still had goals that we wanted to accomplish and did not want the commitment that went along with having a real serious romantic involvement. He was 26 years old and I was 25 years old at the time. He wanted to finish with school and eventually have his own business and that would cost him time and money. I wanted to go back to school and get a college degree in something that would help me get a decent job that would pay me plenty of money so that I would be able to support myself and my kids.

OUR FIRST KISS

When we got to my home, he walked me to the door and we kissed but that was not the only thing he wanted from me. His left hand slipped almost touching my right breast and I moved his hand away. I gently moved his hand away and he got the message that I demanded his respect. I did not allow myself to give in to my desires of inviting him upstairs, (this reservation on my part would serve me well when we finally got serious about spending the rest of our life together.)

OUR SECOND KISS

I did not see him again until that winter when I had heard from his brother that he had had knee surgery and was at Bridgeport recuperating. So, I took the opportunity and went to visit him. I brought him some flowers and some chocolate candy bars and while he lay in bed with his leg up in a hospital bed sling, he looked so vulnerable and defenseless that I just wanted to take him in my arms and cuddle him. I leaned over and kissed him on his lips and found him extremely attractive. I could not help myself from saying to him exactly that, I find you so attractive and I would very much like to see you again. He told me that he also found me attractive and would like to see me when he left the hospital. I spent but a few minutes with him and kissed him again and then said, "See you later."

ACCIDENTAL MEETING... MAYBE NOT

It was a really cold day in March of 1979 and I decided to take my daughter to McDonald's for her birthday. While sitting there enjoying our food, H happened to walk in with his cousin and we said hello to each other as if meeting for the first time.

They both proceeded to sit down in the booth behind the one where the kids and I were sitting. But before he sat down, I noticed that he had a knee brace on that stretched from his thigh down below the knee area and so I asked him, "How are you doing from your leg surgery?" He told me, "I'm doing much better thank you for asking," and he sat down. I had been sitting there with a male friend who had given me and the kids a ride to McDonalds and so in my estimation he didn't want to interrupt and so we did not talk much after those few words.

As I was leaving the restaurant, I turned around and said goodbye to him and his cousin because this time I was not really sure that I would be seeing him again. It felt as if what we both had intimately shared in that hospital room had been soon forgotten.

THIS TIME IT'S FOR REAL

We were destined to be meet and get married. It was a late afternoon on a summer day four months later when I saw him again. As soon as I walked into the place where he had been sitting down already at a table at the far end of the club, he saw me and I saw him and our eyes connected. We could not stop looking at each other as I approached the table. Then, I deliberately sat right next to him. He had been sitting there with one of his many girlfriends and I had walked in with that same male friend, (who was madly in love with me but I was not interested in him that way at all.) I met him at his father's restaurant when I'd go for my tuna fish sandwich during lunch when I was attending school for my GED.

That day would be the beginning of a beautiful romantic life, filled with indescribable friendship, love and affection for each other, and great intimacy. After being in the club for several hours, he asked me in front of his girlfriend and the guy that I was with, "Do you want to get out of the club and go somewhere" and I said "Yes." We left without saying a word to our friends. He took me to a neighborhood bar where his older brother would spend most of his weekends because his girlfriend was the bartender.

We spent the night drinking and talking and hanging out with them. I needed a job and he asked me to work with him at his place and I jumped at the chance of spending more time with him. I said yes. He took me home and I invited him in but he slept in the living room on the sofa and I slept in my bedroom (this would later also serve me well when he finally decides to ask me to marry him.) Get the wisdom. And from that day forward, we continued to spend more time with each other.

COMMITTED TO EACH OTHER

It took three years for him to decide to make me his real and only girlfriend. There were some clinches in this relation-ship in the beginning and I knew that before it would become a stable relationship my children and I would have to go through some things. There were some unsettling moments in our lives that would haunt me for some time.

I knew that in order for me to be his only real girlfriend that I would have to join his world for a while because he was a single man and had no family responsibilities like I did. I would have to choose to live in his world until he was ready for a serious commitment so for over a year my life and my children's lives would be unstable.

I started to work at the bar during the evening shift and would get home in the early morning hours and babysitting had become a problem so I gave my daughter to my sister to keep for several months and then to my grandparents for a few more months. My son went with his father, all the while neglecting my duties as a mother. I finally realized that I could no longer live like that nor do that to my children so I rented my own apartment and quit working at the bar and got my children back. By that time, he had realized that he did want to commit to our relationship so he bought himself a business (a liquor store) and then we moved in together.

I married this man 10 years after our first encounter and I loved him with every being in my body. He was smart, handsome, sexy, a great lover, an excellent father to my two children and our son, a good provider, and the best companion I ever had. I enjoyed everything about him and there was nothing I would have changed about him. H showed me a better way of life and to live a life of abundance.

I can truly say that with him I knew what it was to live a happy and prosperous life, never having to lack for anything. We liked going to Disney World every summer with the kids and to New York for sightseeing anytime we were in the mood. There wasn't a day that he and I didn't get intimate. We just loved being around each other and in each other's arms, hugging and kissing. I would tell the kids, "You kids have nothing to worry about because dad and I will never ever get a divorce." I will always treasure and love this man. He died 14 years after we said to each other, I do.

CHAPTER 9

IT'S A QUESTION MARK

"So now I am giving you a new commandment: Love each other. Just as I have loved you, you should love each other. ³⁵ Your love for one another will prove to the world that you are my disciples."

John 13:34-35 (NLT)

WHAT'S MY STORY WITH C?

"God don't like ugly"

C had his own gutter business and was into installing seamless gutters like rain catchers, you know those metal things that hang off of the eaves or roof edge of a house to keep the rain away from the house, protecting its foundation. He said he had a high school diploma/GED. He also shared that he was divorced and that the nine-year old daughter was from this second marriage. Sometimes she would accompany him to the work sites when he picked her up from school.

He ate out a lot since he was always on the road doing job estimates and meeting potential customers and buying materials for his personal business. I felt that I wanted to take care of him as I had for H. I thought that having a woman to cook for him would keep him away from eating out so much, just saying.

WHY C?

I truly believed that God had arranged for me to meet C and that he had been a 'godsend', as bizarre as it may sound I actually did believe it. I never mentioned it to anyone, you know how crazy that might have sounded.

In my finite mind I thought that he met all the specifications in my new companion that I had requested from God. I was either desperate, stupid or was losing my mind.

When I compared my lifestyle to C's lifestyle there was a huge comparison. I had it all together.

There was nothing really exceptional about him and there was nothing of great significance that he could offer me, except maybe his companionship. I told myself that if I married C I'd help build him up to my standard of living and by putting our resources together we would do well economically.

He lived in a one-bedroom apartment in an area of the city known for drug dealing with local bars on every corner. He told me, that his business had made about $300,000 the year we met. He said to me, I am a single man, what would I need a big house for? I thought who was I to question where he wanted to live. I know that I was not going to live there. I thought that maybe I could've encouraged him to go back to school and get a college education and eventually help me run my business.

MY FAMOUS DEBATE:
TO DATE OR NOT TO DATE C?

I began to debate within myself whether or not I wanted to go ahead with the relationship I was having with C. Deep down inside, I wanted more out of life. I was living in my own home in a quiet neighborhood in a decent town, where in my living room alone I could have fit two of his rooms. I was making a great salary, driving in a brand new car and I didn't lack for anything.

I have to admit that I wasn't drawn to him immediately but I felt a pull, an unnatural pull to seek his attention. It was not his looks or his manners that attracted me to him, it was hard to explain. I can't remember exactly what attracted me to him except the thought of him being H in spirit. On one end my thoughts would tell me to stop seeing him then on the other end my thoughts would say things like, stop thinking of yourself better and more righteous and don't look down on him, he has a good heart and listen to what the people are saying about him being a "good man." I was more confused than a blind bat.

I liked that he had confessed falling in love with me. It also helped make up my mind about him when I thought about him having his own business which meant financially I'd have no worries. That encouraged me a lot. He appeared on the surface to have good business sense and he talked about all the jobs he'd have lined up for the year and I saw the money rolling in. And I couldn't discount that he had demonstrated time and time again that he was a 'good man' with me, my family, and his children. He was attending church on Sundays and that was a plus. So, I ended the debate and decided to stay in the relationship and see where it would take me.

WHAT GOT INTO ME?

I thought a lot about that house by the lake and I figured that if I stayed, eventually I would get that house. I diluted myself with the thought of being wealthy. That it didn't matter that I was not in love with C. I figured that I would learn to love him with time. I had not realized that I was headed down a sinful path. I must have been blinded by pride and greed not to see what I was doing and where I was headed. But believe me when I tell you, I didn't recognize that woman that was residing in me, she was not me. I don't know who that woman was that was behaving in such an ungodly fashion. In the secular world there is a saying and it's repeated by some church people, "God don't like ugly," meaning that ungodly behavior is frowned upon by God.

CHAPTER 10

VANITY

"Keep watch and pray, so that you will not give in to temptation. For the spirit is willing, but the body is weak!" Matthew 26:41 (NLT)

I'M STILL ATTRACTIVE

"I was flirting with sin and had no idea what I was preparing myself for..."

About six months after burying my dear beloved husband, I had noticed how much weight I had lost and I wasn't quite sure why it happened. But I went from a size ten to a six in a matter of three months. I felt that I needed to tone my body so I went to the Sports Authority athletic store and bought an elliptical machine, a workout bench and some weights. I was working out on a daily basis on the elliptical machine and began to see the results as I lost more weight. So, I decided to stop using the machine but I continued to use the weights. I noticed that I had toned up quite a bit. I was much more physically active taking daily walks during my breaks at work, climbing eight flights of stairs several times and not breaking a sweat. I started to feel rejuvenated again. I was still very much attractive and in great shape. I dressed up in beautiful dresses with high heels for church and work, and kept up with the latest fashions.

I guess that in the back of my mind I thought that one day I might like to meet someone and get married a few years down the road. I never thought that I would be meeting someone only fifteen months later and marry that person after eighteen months of becoming a widow but there I was, flirting.

I ENJOYED FLIRTING

I began to look forward to meeting with him at Home Depot. I would get there before him and hide in one of the aisles and wait from a distance to see which entrance he would use. I wanted to see the look of anticipation on his face because he was going to see me; was my assumption. It had become so obvious that he looked forward to seeing me by the way he met me as soon as I'd call him, and in some strange way I looked forward to seeing him. When I say strange, I mean that my heart did not leap for joy when seeing him and I didn't have butterflies in my stomach over it. It was weird.

C was a medium-dark skinned 5'7 tall man. He barely had a neck and his body was pear shape, (my estimation). His arms were shorter than his torso and they swayed as he walked, and he had a protruding belly with a small waist. When he walked, he would wobble side to side and if he walked fast he'd look like he was hopping, leaning his body to the left. He wore his hair spiked up with gel. He wore trendy prescription smoke-colored lens with silver rimmed eyeglasses that hid his fatty eyelids and protruding eyes. As soon as I'd see C walk into Home Depot I'd come out and wave and signal for him to meet me half way. Then I would turn around and parade myself in front of him so he'd notice as I moved. I'd wear tight-fitting jeans with high heels to show my figure. I always made sure to refresh my make-up before our meetings. He'd show up with a wide smile on his face. I still had no idea as to why I was behaving this way or what I was preparing myself for. I'd find out one year later.

INVITATION TO FIRST RESTAURANT

In September, a month after we'd met C called me at work one afternoon and asked me, would you like to go out to dinner with me this evening? I said, "Yes I'd like that but you would have to meet me in Norwalk I am working a few hours there after work at the Women's Crisis Center." I was doing my internship in a domestic violence crisis center for my Master's Program. Then he said, there is a restaurant in that town I'd like to take you to. I was so excited that I was going on my first real date with him.

When we met at the restaurant, he opened the door and grabbed my elbow to usher me into the restaurant. As we were walking into the place, I noticed that he stumbled a few times so I asked him, what was the matter? And he said, I bought these shoes today and I did not try them on at the store. I think they're a size too big. I thought that was weird. We sat down for dinner and I ordered a blackened salmon with baked potato and steamed vegetables. I had a glass of White Zinfandel; I don't remember what he ordered.

During dessert, I started the conversation about how important my children and grandchildren were to me. I love my children and grandchildren so much and I don't want anything coming between us. I also explained to him, I am not looking for anyone to get serious with at this moment but if that time comes that person would have to accept my family because they are very important to me. C told me the same about his children. He said, "my children are very important to me and we have a good relationship. If the woman I am seeing doesn't like them then I can't be with that woman." I noticed that he spoke only when I initiate the conversation. Otherwise, we'd sit there in silence.

ANNOYED BUT FLATTERED

After dinner, he escorted me to my car, again holding me by my elbow which made me feel uncomfortable because I have never been held by my elbow before and it felt weird. That week at work, I asked my colleague who I believed was more familiar with Hispanic customs and she told me that he was being a gentleman by escorting me by my elbow as we walked. Ooh! I thought. He then reached over to kiss me but I pulled away from him and thought, he thinks that buying me dinner cost a kiss; I was turned off by his gesture. I told him, I am not ready, it's too soon, we had only known each other less than a month. When I got to my car, he tried to kiss me again and I told him right out, I'm not going to kiss every man that takes me out on a date. I had to be very clear with him and explain what I wanted out of a relationship.

I thought it had been a bad idea going out on a date with him; maybe I had given him the wrong message. I told him, I would not go out with him again. I thought that it had been silly to have gone out with him in the first place. I rambled on about my future and marriage. I knew then that I wanted to get married again but it had to be done right and with the right person. I told him, in the event that I do get married again it would have to be with a godly man, who loved God more than life, attend church regularly and read the Bible. C looked at me and told me, I attend a local church in Bridgeport and I understand where you stand on your beliefs, the marriage vows are important to me too!

That night we left and went our separate ways. As I was driving home C called me from his cell phone to tell me, he had fallen in love with me. I thought that was weird but I felt flattered at the same. I did not respond to his confession except to say, goodnight.

I WAS IMPRESSED

Two weeks later I invited him to lunch to discuss the business at Señor Salsa in Fairfield. They serve good Mexican food, to discuss the business. I liked that he showed himself reliable and dependable as he came to my assistance every time I called him. I liked the attention that he gave me and it pleased me. I found his knowledge of tools and materials that the shop needed for the repairs fascinating. As our meetings to Home Depot became more and more frequent, almost daily, I had developed an attraction toward him that had nothing to do with emotions. It was a strange type of attraction, might have been because he was always so willing to help me since I was a widow in need. I actually did like all the attention I was getting from him.

He began to send me flowers at work. The floral bouquets were a huge assortment of wild beautiful colorful flowers. Some arrangements came with stuffed animals, such as teddy bears, cats and dogs. And a note expressing his attraction toward me. I can't remember what he wrote in them.

MY HEAD IN A WHIRLWIND

In the middle of September, he invited my family and I to The New England State Exposition in West Springfield Massachusetts. He paid for everything, including the mid-way rides and the food. He was a big hit with my family. My family had so much fun and they were very grateful to him for bringing them there. I met his two teenage children for the first time as well, and I enjoyed their company as they were always hanging onto their dad, hugging and kissing him.

I had been there before with H and the family and it was always so much fun because there were always new things to see. He ended up going back a week later, he invited me to go but I did not.

The weeks were going by so fast that my head was in a whirlwind and I was feeling an attraction toward C that kept getting stronger and stronger, but I wasn't in love with him.

One day, I finally asked him if he didn't mind taking over buying the materials for the shop and I handed him my Home Depot credit card. I needed to trust him at that time because I had started my second semester at school and was too busy with my fulltime job, school and internship that I didn't have time to go by the business nor buy materials for it. I was glad that he agreed to take full charge of the business and oversee all the work. I could only come by on Saturdays to see the progress while the workers were there and I got a chance to chat with them about the work and to thank them.

I WAS ADMIRED AND LOVED

October rolled around and C continued to send me flowers at work once a week. He'd call me every day to tell me about his love for me. He'd say things like, "I love a woman like you and I can't wait to see you after work." It felt good to be admired and desired and I enjoyed every moment of it. Although he had confessed to have fallen in love with me, I chose to treat him as a friend and business associate. He was just someone helping me with getting the business underway by overseeing its progress. I kept on meeting him at Home Depot near the building supplies area.

My life was busy by now and C was very persistent about taking me out on dates. I found these dates a distraction and I had a full schedule that I had to stick with because obtaining my Masters' degree was a mandate from God; I couldn't mess that up.

One evening I gave in to his request and agreed to go out with him. We went out on several more dates after that. He would take me the movies, more dinner dates and to lunch on occasions to discuss the progress of the shop. One day when we were out looking for a specific restaurant that C said served great steaks, he asked me while at a stop sign, how old I was? We had been dating for some six weeks and I thought it strange that he would ask me then. When I told him, I'm about to turn fifty-one, his head made a double take, his eyebrows went up, his eyes opened very wide and the expression on his face and body gesture were quite odd, his forehead wrinkled, his mouth made a downward frown, and he moved away from me as if he had seen a ghost. Then he told me "I thought I would never go out with a woman older than me because I like them younger than me." He continued to say, I thought that you were like forty something, but it's too late, I've fallen in love with you, and your age doesn't matter because you don't look like you're in your fifties. I responded, "It's not too late to stop seeing me because there is no obligation and you don't have to continue to date me." He told me, "I don't want to stop dating you" and then he looked down at my legs and he made a comment about them, "what beautiful legs you have" (I wore skirts most of the time when I was dating him.) He would always make comments about my legs and about how pretty my face was.

We finally found the restaurant and had a good night out; eating and talking about things we enjoy and what things were not pleasing to God. We were still not kissing at this time, and I didn't want to put myself out there because I had to remember that I was a Christian woman and I had to respect my God. I was fearful of doing something sinful in the eyes of God.

CHAPTER 11

THE DILEMMA

"Dear brothers and sisters, ʲwhen troubles of any kind come your way, consider it an opportunity for great joy. For you know that when your faith is tested, your endurance has a chance to grow. So let it grow, for when your endurance is fully developed, you will be perfect and complete, needing nothing." James 1:2-4 (NLT)

LACK OF DISCERNMENT

"The complexities of our lives will create everlasting consequences that will either empower or hinder us."

I had other opportunities to date other men, especially in my church since everyone knew that I was a widow. There was one particular member in church that I liked and most times our eyes would meet and we'd stare at each other for a while, smile and keep on walking. There were several men at work that were interested but only for an adulterous affair that I was not available for, as it is a sin. In school there was a very handsome man that I would admire from a distance never gave in to any temptation to approach him.

As I mentioned before there was that church brother that I would often catch looking at me and I'd pretend I hadn't noticed him until one day I actually stared (intently) back. He was the most handsome black man in the church. He actually looked interested, because he looked at me with that intense look, even when we were singing hymns he'd turn around and look at me and he'd catch me looking at him. He reminded me of H a lot.

At first I thought that he was the one God had chosen for me. He was about 6'1 (in my estimation), slim with a tan complexion, handsome and a great dresser. He was attending graduate school for his Doctorate degree in Social Work. I knew this because the pastor had mentioned it earlier that year and had asked him to think about supervising a program geared toward young men being released from prison. I had the misfortune to learn something I wish I had not learned about him at a church function on a very cold October night. It was a dinner celebration for one of our longtime church member who had just retired from her job after 30 plus years and was moving away to another state, twelve hundred miles away.

When I entered the building I ran into my church admirer in the foyer as we both were standing at the coat check-in line waiting for the lady to take our coats and when he saw me he smiles I smiled back. We both said, hello, how are you, at the same time. I thought that was awkward. He went into the ballroom before I did and I thought I had lost him because the place was crowded with people.

The place was sparkly with chandeliers on the ceilings, white linen cloth tables filled with crystal clear stem wine glasses and shiny silverware. Everyone was looking so festive in their gowns and the men in their suits, lovely I thought. I walked in looking for my assigned table and when I got there, he was sitting down and there was an empty chair next to him. So I was excited about the seating arrangement and thought, could this be the man that God has chosen for me and all along I was thinking that it was the gutter guy.

FALSE PERCEPTION

I greeted everyone sitting at the table with a smile and a "God bless you." I took my seat and then I greeted him and we made small talk about the church member that was retiring. The Pastor then mentioned that he was not just celebrating her retirement and farewell but her birthday as well, and asked everyone to sing "Happy Birthday" to her. So that started him and I talking about birthdays and I told him that I also celebrated my birthday in October and then he told me, my girlfriend also celebrates her birthday in October. I was shocked to hear that.

There I was thinking that he liked me since he had been giving me that impression for several weeks. His stares were seductive and enticing and so I thought I had a chance with him, but I was wrong. So I continued to make small talk with him and when it was all over, I excused myself from the table and left the banquet hall.

THOUGHTLESSNESS

I was angry with myself for my foolish behavior and how things turned out that night. I got in my car and instead of driving home I called C and asked him, what he was doing? He said, "I'm watching television", and I told him, "I'm coming over," he said "sure." I had told God that I liked that church member but if he was not the one for me then God would give me a sign and at that moment, I thought well he has a girlfriend so he must not be the one. I thought God had answered my prayers so it has to be C that God has chosen for me.

I couldn't drive my car any faster that night without getting a traffic ticket. It had to be C since he had the spirit of H in him, so I was convinced of that! In my anger and haste I made a decision that would gravely cost me a great deal. I was obviously not thinking in my right mind. I had taken the wrong direction and that detour would prove disastrous and would negatively impact not only my life but the lives of my love ones. I went chasing the desires of my flesh and drove right into the hands of Satan.

IMPRUDENT

When I got to his apartment, he was happy to see me. He was literally shaking all over and it wasn't cold in the apartment. I think it was the joy of me being there, by my estimation, and his smile almost left the sides of his mouth it was so wide. He escorted me to the living room and offered me the sofa to sit on and he threw himself on the chaise that was directly across from the sofa.

The living room was so small that both pieces of furniture touched and I was practically face to face with C when I sat down. He had on a house robe, no pajamas because I could see his chest and his bare legs. I don't remember what our conversation was about that night. I do remember that I was feeling very vulnerable, angry, betrayed and lonely; I wanted to be with someone. Knowing what could've happened I got up to leave when he started to get up to escort me out. That's when his robe opened up exposing his slightly haired chest. I looked up at him and our eyes met and I fell into his arms and we kissed for the first time. I knew that if I stayed in his apartment a moment longer, I might have ended up having sex with him so I forced myself up from the chaise and said, goodnight. He didn't want me to leave by the grip he had on my hand. But I was determined to leave and sin was the farthest thing in my mind that night.

PREDICAMENT

I went home that night but it was too late for I was feeling aroused and could not stop the feeling. It would've been better not to have felt anything. To have stayed away from touching one another and waited a little longer until we both were sure of what we were getting into. I knew that something had been awakened in me and I was too vulnerable to tame it because at that point I wanted to be held and loved.

I realized that I had to be extra careful not to be alone with him whenever we had to discuss the shop's progress and especially when we went out to dinner. I told myself not to visit his home unless his children were visiting.

In my anger I guess I became arrogant, I don't know. I was still trying to figure out what I was doing. Understand that when we take matters into our own hands and stand against

God's will, we will lose. I will understand that concept a little too late. I did not have a well thought-out plan and in my haste I would end up destroying what I had.

RAMIFICATIONS

I was a professional working for the Department of Mental Health and had consulted many clients who had a family member die. But I refused to seek professional help for myself. I remember a close friend had given me a few books on the grieving process and I tossed them because they reminded me of my loss.

It was not until much later that I saw what my haste to get my wants and desires met had caused me. Only by then it was much too late to take back what I had started and there had been too much collateral damage in both my personal life as well as in the lives of my adult children and grandchildren. The complexities of life will create everlasting consequences in our lives that will either empower or hinder us.

CHAPTER 12

DEVASTATION

"All praise to God, the Father of our Lord Jesus Christ. God is our merciful Father and the source of all comfort. ⁴He comforts us in all our troubles so that we can comfort others. When they are troubled, we will be able to give them the same comfort God has given us."

2 Corinthians 1:3-4 (NLT)

GOD FORGIVE ME...

During the most vulnerable moment in my life I had lost sight of what was most important for my soul and my whole being, my first true love, God. I use the word true because I once was truly and deeply in love with my God and I never thought nor imagined that I would find myself actually looking away from Him and forgetting all that He had been to my family and me. My God who had given me favor and my Savior who had kept me from the pit of hell. I allowed my grief over the death of my husband to take precedence over God's love, comfort and peace. No matter how much I wanted to feel God's peace and comfort, the pain was much more than what I could bare.

I obviously was not vigilant enough in my spiritual walk with God to have fallen "from grace" so easy and quick. I know that this could have happened to the most faithful of servants of the Lord. I have read many stories. I know it was foolish of me to think that I was "invincible" and that it would never happen to me, but it did. I know that I did not give up on God at that time it was just that I had made several requests of God that I was not ready for and so I became impatient with God and took matters into my own hands. "Patience is a virtue," please take heed. I had strayed away from my moral and values and biblical teachings.

Because I wanted my suffering to go away fast I tried to rush God into changing my grieving situation and make all the pain go away immediately. I gave him an ultimatum. I, His creation dared to give God my creator an ultimatum. What was I thinking? Well, obviously I was not thinking and as a matter of fact, I was not in my right mind at all. I had been betrayed by my own passions for the Kingdom of God for human love and affection.

I COULD NOT BELIEVE HE WAS GONE

"The complexities of the grieving process and the mistakes we have the propensity to make during that process."

During my grief I would only focus on my loss and the pain that I was experiencing. In my despair I began to blame myself as well as God for his death. I blamed myself for not being there at the hospital when the doctors would come and visit, which was usually in the mornings because I would go to work.

I continued to go to work every day since I would come and visit with him in the evening. But by then the doctors would have already left for the day. I thought that because of my constant prayers, he would get well and come home so I believed that everything would be alright.

I then realized after his death that if I had been in the hospital room with him every day especially in the morning hours that I could have talked to the doctors about what other things could have been done for him to keep him alive, like I had done in other cases before when he had been hospitalized. But he never mentioned anything about why he had been losing so much weight, so I left it at that, and did not think about it.

He and I enjoyed our vacation and came home with plenty to talk about regarding the vacation and how we were definitely going to move to the Midwest to be closer to my cousin and her husband since they had established such a good relationship with him. We were both excited about the move after I graduated from school. But then I began to notice that he was not looking well at all and he was not himself anymore. So, I suggested that he go see his doctor.

I drove him to the doctor's office and the doctor took a series of test and told us that he saw on the chest x-ray spots on his lungs and so that doctor referred him to an oncologist who also did a series of tests. The oncologist told us that the x-rays films show he had spots all over his inside, on his lungs and other vital organs and he was sure what they were. This doctor recommended that H make an appointment with a specialist from the Stone-Kettering Clinic in New York City. We immediately contacted the doctor whose name had been given to us and he gave us an appointment but we never went to the appointment in New York City because H ended up in the hospital.

However, the specialist was able to come and examine him at the hospital and he gave him the report that the spots were cancerous tumors that had metastasized throughout his entire body. I was not in that hospital room when the doctors started him on morphine which put him to sleep until he died. I was not made aware of it because I was working. All I know is that he slept the whole time that I visited with him and I never got to hear his voice again the whole six days that he remained in the hospital's hospice ward. I went and sat with him and prayed and some our friends and family members visited and we would pray not realizing that he was dying.

IF ONLY I HAD DONE SOMETHING

The day before he died, I had taken the day off from work to go to the hospital early that morning to tell the doctor to take him off of the medication they had been feeding him to keep him asleep and to start feeding him food through tubes. The doctor told me that my husband had requested to die that way and that he could not change the "patient's request" (Advanced Directive) that H had signed. I never got to say goodbye nor talk to him about my love for him and how much I was going to miss him. I did not get a chance and that haunted me. I hated not having had that chance because I thought that God had it all under control.

I am being very honest when I say that I hated my life and wanted to die (I wasn't thinking suicide.) Not having my beloved husband alive was more than I could bear. But God did have it all under control. I had gone to God in prayer to give me back my husband. I prayed and cried for hours asking God to please give me back my husband and God heard my prayers and answered them.

He had revealed to me that I was to go to the hospital the next day and tell his doctor to remove H from the machine that was feeding him the sleep medication and to start feeding him nutritional foods that would bring him back to health. I went back to the hospital the next morning and told the doctor to stop feeding H the medication drip that kept him asleep and start tube feeding him. The doctor did not have the permission to reverse H's decision to expire that way. There I was telling the doctor to give me back my husband and he had told me no in an indirect way.

I did not know what to do or who to talk to and I just let it be and did not even ask him for advice as to what I was supposed to do because I did not know. I felt like I could not do anything, and that my hands were tied, so I did not question what the doctor told me and left it at that. But I could not tell him what the Lord had told me the night before because I thought that he would not understand anything about my faith. I did not have the nerve to tell that doctor the truth about my God and about His saving grace. That my God answers prayers. I knew what I knew to be true about God but I did not dare share it with that doctor.

I spent the last few hours of his life with him in his room somewhat confused because I knew that it was God's will to give him back to me but I was clueless as to what my rights were as a wife and I didn't know what to do at that point. So I accepted that was what my H wanted and I had to respect his wishes. As much as I wanted him back I thought well, if that was what had to be so be it. I stayed to visit with him since I had taken the day off from work. I was complaining to myself, look at his lips they are so dry and cracked let me wipe them with some water and this Q-tip. As I was wiping his lips he began to grasp as for air and he took his last breath and died.

I walked out to the corridor where I saw a couple of nurses talking to each other behind the counter and told them, I think my husband is dead. The nurses walked over to the room and checked him and one of the nurses called the doctor on duty. She leaned over him and puts the stethoscope over his chest and tells the other nurse, there is no heartbeat. The doctor walks in and knowing why he is there, checks H's chest and declares him dead and the nurse documents the hour he gave her. My beloved H died that morning.

I HATED BEING LEFT ALONE

At first I was numb and then I was so angry with the doctor but more so with myself for not knowing how to handle that situation. Several years later I was told by a friend of mine who happens to be a nurse that I could have gone to the hospital administrators and requested to have his Advanced Directive revoked. I never got to say goodbye to my lover and my friend, nor tell him how much I was going to miss him.

H IS REALLY GONE

He was viewed at Prince of Peace Funeral Home on Washington Avenue in Bridgeport. It's a small building in comparison to other funeral homes I've visited. It only has two viewing rooms and a foyer and it was elbow to elbow, that's how many people were there to pay their respect to H. His aunts who attended his church did the Rosary but I was not in the room during that time.

I did not want to sit in the same room with my deceased husband. I never approached the casket the entire time I was there because I didn't want his dead image in my mind. Most of the time I was standing in the foyer with my church family and never once did I seek out my daughter to see how she was doing. I was too loaded with Xanax to even think or feel for that matter. I was just there in body. I went into the viewing room only when my church Elder went in to say a farewell speech and he kept using the wrong last name from another member from our church. I know that he came because I asked him to but I really should have called his Parish Priest to come and give the last word.

However, several of the church members had visited H in the hospital and they did show up at the funeral for my sake. I don't remember anything else about that night. I don't remember much about getting up the next day for the funeral nor how I got to the church for the service. I know that there was no eulogy and the service went by quick and then down to the cemetery.

His Priest did not go and I felt awful afterward because he had been a member for fourteen years and that Priest had married us. But I was not the one who made the funeral arrangements, instead I handed that charge to H's youngest brother. The last thing I would've wanted was for the funeral director to preside at H's funeral. It should have been his Priest. There was no typical hysteria or crying and falling out coming from me. That's usual for Hispanic women at funerals, especially when the casket is being lowered down into the gravesite and so no one thought to console me because I appeared to be alright and in control.

Not really; it was the Xanax. If I regret anything about his death, it was the lack of mourning that I denied myself and not showing the pain of that great loss. I wanted to be strong for my daughter and grandchildren and didn't want them to see me fall apart. In their eyes, grandmother had to be strong. What a foolish thing that was to do and keep back my tears and suffering just because I wanted to prove something to somebody.

ABANDONED

At the house, all of H's brothers and their families, including our longtime friends are gathered downstairs in his brother's home. Meantime, my brothers and sisters and my personal friends are upstairs in my home. I'm not sure how long they were with me when my brother tells me that he and the others were going to my youngest sister's place. I turn to him and asked, why are you leaving me so soon? I'm the one that needs you all. I'm the one whose husband has just been buried. But they all walked out without a word. Everyone else that was downstairs left without saying goodbye.

WHERE WERE MY TRUE FRIENDS?

I felt alone and was suffering all by myself and of all the friends I thought I had none would actually call me to find out how I was doing or if I needed something. I was always the one to call them and ask them how they and their families were doing. I mean we were longtime friends of twenty plus years whose kids had grown up together from when they were toddlers.

These friends and their children attended every party I ever had from birthdays to weddings, to baptisms to graduation celebrations, and they all took flight when my late husband died. I received no phone calls for months from any of these friends.

MOVE ON WITH MY LIFE

At that moment, I had made up my mind to stay focused and be a mother to my adult children and a grandmother to my darling grandkids. I was going to finish school with my Master's degree in Social Work and live the life that I was meant to live according to the will of God. There was a plan I was called to do for the Kingdom of God and I needed my degree, I had seen the vision. I chose to be obedient and go ahead with the plans that were before.

No matter how much I wanted to feel God's peace and comfort, the pain was much more than I could bear. I pretended that I was doing alright emotionally and mentally for the sake of my children and grandchildren. I felt that I had to be strong for them. I would not cry in front of them and would laugh and appeared as if everything was going good. I kept telling myself, you are a strong person and you need to move on with your life. I was determined that I would not allow anyone nor any-thing to stop me.

I finally came to the realization that knowing God intimately, attending church, serving the church, and living a godly life will not prevent a believer from dying but most importantly that we learn to depend on God while we're alive. That God will be with us throughout our trials and tribulations until we see Him face to face. We are only passing through this world for this is not our home; our real home is in heaven. God revealed to me that H is in heaven.

But in my quiet room, I thought that I would have no relief from all this pain and suffering. It was depressing. All throughout my childhood and into my adult life. I would ask myself the question, was I destined to cry forever and ever and never have a moments rest from crying. I had suffered so much in this life that I could only feel pity for myself. Ever since I could remember I had been crying from one painful moment to another.

.

CHAPTER 13

BROKEN RELATIONSHIPS

"¹⁶All Scripture is inspired by God and is useful to teach us what is true and to make us realize what is wrong in our lives. It corrects us when we are wrong and teaches us to do what is right. ¹⁷God uses it to prepare and equip his people to do every good work." 2 Timothy 3:16-17 (NLT)

CHILDHOOD RELATIONSHIP

I grew up in East Harlem, also known as Spanish Harlem and El Barrio in upper Manhattan, New York City, during the early1960'. I was a toddler when my parents moved to New York City from Puerto Rico in 1956. Growing up poor with alcoholic parents created in me major insecurities and emotional issues. Those were unstable times for me.

My parents would disappear every now and then leaving me and my siblings with whoever was around at the time, maybe a friend, or maybe a family member. My parents for the most part were habitual drinkers and fighting was routine and that image destroyed any pleasant memory I could have had of them. On some occasions there would lamps flying through the air when they were trying to hit each other and we'd have to duck or get hit with one of those flying objects. I remember the broken glass all over the floor and being careful not to cut my little feet. And, the times that mom, me and my sibling would have to run into the street in the middle of the night in pure winter, without coats to escape the madness. The foul language and indecent things that I witnessed as a young child should never have happened. I did not hate my parents. I hated their lifestyle. Many times I wished that I had been born into a different family. I have suffered brokenness due to childhood sexual abuse, parental neglect, and abandonment.

Unbeknownst to those who know me, those experiences had caused emotional and mental instability in me for a long time. Those childhood memories were a constant torment. The fear of being abandoned, abused and neglected have been a constant companion.

Early childhood relationships for the most part affected how I related in later years. I hated living alone and so I was always seeking attention, affection, and love from everyone and unfortunately, my heart was always being broken into pieces because I asked far too much of people. I had several failed relationships with man because I demanded more from the relationship than they could give, such as affection, something that my mom and pop never gave me.

The man had to be the leader in the home and make the most money, that's what I expected of a man. I had to get all the attention from that man because of my issues with neglect and abandonment. I demanded protection and security from him. I believe that if I was going to give of myself I wanted my needs met as well. I did not want to share my man with anyone and I refused to be disrespected. I was not perfect far from it. That is why I am so glad that God chose a wretch like me and cleansed me of all filth and slime that had pulled me down into the gutter and He brought me out "white as snow."

Purify me from my sins, and I will be clean; wash me, and I will be whiter than snow. Psalm 51:7

EXPECTATION OF THE HISPANIC FEMALE RELATIONSHIP

Patterns of relationships are formed early in life through our culture and beliefs. Like many women who grew up in Hispanic homes, the expectations were that women get married, take care of the man, the home, and the children. The Hispanic family puts a strong emphasis on family. For me growing up in a Hispanic family meant following in the steps of those women before me.

I was born in Puerto Rico but raised in the United States. The females in my time and in my culture were taught to be the caregivers and nurturers in the family. That was what I knew. For the most part, the Hispanic females were groomed for marriage as soon as they hit puberty. At that time, the mothers would begin to prepare their daughters to get marry and have babies. In addition, the cultural belief was that women who don't get married will end up old maids. That thought was always in the back of most Hispanic female's minds and most do end up getting married, even if the male they choose is not the right one. The reasoning behind it is that they don't end up alone but always have a male companion. But times have changed and the Hispanic female takes longer to find her mate and get married. But for the most part, they do marry.

"Don't copy the behavior and customs of this world, but let God transform you into a new person by changing the way you think. Then you will learn to know God's will for you, which is good and pleasing and perfect"
Romans 12:2 (NLT)

MY DAUGHTER AND I

However, I had taught my daughter to get a college education before marriage. I also taught her how to be a good wife when she did marry, since it's the Hispanic thing to do; pass it down. My expectations of my daughter was that she attends college and experience life first as a single adult and then get married and start a family.

I recall this one time when she was 18 years old, and I took her with a couple of her friends to see her favorite singer, at the time George Lamont, perform at a nightclub and when he got off the stage I followed him with my eyes to see where he was headed and I grabbed her arm and took her to meet him as he was coming out of the kitchen where he had gone for a repose. That's the kind of mother I was with my daughter. My daughter and I had a special kind of relationship and I would do anything for her, within reason because I was still the mother. When she got married, I'd invite her and her husband to our friend's annual Christmas party and I'd take her shopping for an outfit to wear. I'd buy her fancy dresses to wear to any event even though she was married. I enjoyed buying her things. I didn't care how much it cost but she had to look beautiful and most of the time, she was the prettiest lady at the party or event.

When I went to give birth to my daughter I took a taxi cab to the hospital, Metropolitan Hospital in Manhattan, New York City, from the Bronx all by myself. I don't know how I made it from one borough to the other and did not give birth in the cab. Her father was not home at the time. The next day, in the late afternoon, he came to the room to see me. I was afraid of him because he abused me physically and I thought he would hit me for coming to the hospital without him. I took her home by myself. It was horrible living with her father and I hated it. I remember always singing to her as she was growing up this song:

"You and me against the world,
Sometimes it seems like you and me against the world,
When all the others turn their backs and walked away,
You can count on me to stay.
Remember when the circus came to town
How you were frightened by the clown,
Wasn't it nice to be around someone that you knew,
Someone who was big and strong and looking out for
You and me against the world,
Sometimes it seems like you and me against the world
And for all the times we've cried I always felt that
God was on our side.
And when one of us is gone,
And one of us is left to carry on,

Then remembering will have to do,
Our memories alone will get us through
Think about the days of me and you,
Of you and me against the world."

Sung by Helen Redding.
Released June 17, 1974
Capitol Records

My mom had been dead for six months and my pops was drinking himself to death, (he lived to be 75 years old. Mom died at 56.) So, I found myself alone in an abusive relationship. But one day I packed up my belongings and moved to Bridgeport CT to stay with my older brother while I found an apartment for me and my 2-year-old. It was always my girl and me. I have the 3 adult children but it will always be her and I. I know that I have not been the world's greatest mom but I did try considering how I was raised. Raising a child back then did not come with a manual. It was do the best you can. H coming into our lives was the best thing that could have happened for us both. He was the father she never had. Her father was killed by a subway train in NYC, when he felled onto the tracks as the train was approaching.

As my life became stable she was able to reap the benefits of all H offered in our relationship. We enjoyed many vacations together. She and I went out to dinners and movies together. We'd go shopping until we dropped. New York was our favorite place to shop for school clothes and she was the best dressed female student in middle and high school. I would volunteer to watch the girls for her when she and her husband went out to dinner, movies, or his job banquets. I helped her whenever she asked me but for the most part she would ask 'dad'. She and her dad developed such a strong bond that there was nothing that he wouldn't do for her. Her dad and I took turns being in the delivery room when she had the second and third child.

When dad died our lives changed. I started working overtime and was hardly ever around because I didn't want to be home. It was too painful for me. I would come home to sleep only. I was still around for her to help with the girls and the house. I remember that she wanted to paint two of the girls' rooms and I offered to help buy the paint and the border as well as the bed comforter and matching sheet sets. I gave the oldest child a bedroom set that belonged to H and me. I was around for the girl's birthday parties and I continued to by their outfits for the annual family portrait that we took during the Christmas holidays.

But when I met C the strong bond that I had with my daughter began to unravel. I started to spent more time on myself and got too involved with the business. I started to go on more dates with C and take week long vacations outside the state. I rarely visited since I had work, school, and the new relationship, as well as working all the overtime that I was offered, plus the internships. That distanced between us put a damper on our relationship. When she remarries it compounds the distance even more. We both are remarried and living different lives. When I tried to come back into her life again there was a strong pull from her new husband to keep us apart. I understood his dilemma and made up in my mind to keep the peace with my daughter and spent time with her as much as was allowed. I couldn't ask for anything more. But my moving away to Texas only made it worse in trying to reestablish my relationship with her being so far away. There were many times when my daughter and I did not see eye to eye but I love her dearly. I am so proud of the woman she has become.

MY GRANDCHILDREN AND ME

I would take all four granddaughters and my daughter and my only grandson, (from my youngest son) at the time shopping for Christmas outfits to take our annual family portrait. I enjoyed picking out the girl's fancy holiday dresses in red velvet with black satin skirts or gold satin with black velvet skirts with all the holiday glitter. I'd put pretty fancy ribbons in their hair; the pearl necklaces and earrings, they had to have them; it was a must. And, my grandson with his shirt and bowtie stood out among all the girls. At home I'd have a drawer full of candy and I'd make sure that it was always full of all sorts of candies and chocolates. How I enjoyed spoiling my grandchildren. But, I was also a disciplinarian and they knew not to cross the line because I was serious about it but for the most part, they were all good kids. Then they grew up. I will always make myself available for my loved ones and they know that I will always love them until God calls me home.

C AND HIS PARENT RELATIONSHIP

I can't remember where we were headed, I happened to ask C about his parents. He began crying when he was telling me about his father having died two months before we met. He said, "My mom and him divorced years ago when I was five years old. She left him and went back to Puerto Rico to take care of her elderly parents who were sick."

His story touched my heart because it brought back memories about my own childhood experiences about a time when we were separated from my parents every so often. My youngest sister and I are sitting with pops, at a train station, waiting for the train to arrive and I can remember his sad face. It was always his job to deliver us girls to my older sister's home in Connecticut when mom had her nervous breakdowns and he had to work and there was no one to watch us. I remember waking up in a car (taxi) which brought us to her home from the station. I could never remember when he would leave. I know that both me and my youngest sister would run to the window of the bedroom that night and cry out for "mommy" but she would never come for us. I never remember how I got into bed but I'd wake up in it the next day. Everything else would be a fog.

I WAS LOOKING FOR A RELATIONSHIP

Although C and I had been seeing each other more and more I was still not sure if I wanted this relationship to get serious. But then he would flatter me again with his words and I'd think about it some more. For example, I don't remember how we got started talking about C's ex-wives but it must have been on one of our driving excursions to a restaurant maybe. He went on a tangent (which was unusual) about his divorce to the mother of his children and his lack of trust for women but that with me it was different because I was a God-fearing woman. He felt that he could trust me. He wanted a woman who knew what stability was all about, since he knew that I had been in the same relationship for twenty-four years and he liked that I was stable. He wanted a woman who worked and knew how to handle a household and a family. A woman that would help the man take care of their home, and seek to educate herself and aspire for better things; and especially that would love his children. So of course the nurturer and caregiver nature in me kicked into high gear and I felt chosen to serve this man who in my mind needed to be taken care of.

CHAPTER 14

SLAVES TO SINS

"Because of the weakness of your human nature, I am using the illustration of slavery to help you understand all this. Previously, you let yourselves be slaves to impurity and lawlessness, which led ever deeper into sin. Now you must give yourselves to be slaves to righteous living so that you will become holy. When you were slaves to sin, you were free from the obligation to do right. ²¹ And what was the result? You are now ashamed of the things you used to do, things that end in eternal doom. But now you are free from the power of sin and have become slaves of God. Now you do those things that lead to holiness and result in eternal life. For the wages of sin is death, but the free gift of God is eternal life through Christ Jesus our Lord." Romans 6:19-23 (NLT)

THE NIGHT OF SIN

"Come now, let's settle this," says the LORD. "Though your sins are like scarlet, I will make them as white as snow. Though they are red like crimson, I will make them as white as wool. Isaiah 1:18 (NLT)

The night that would bring my world crumbling down. A night that I would regret for a lifetime. A night that will teach me a lesson that I will never forget, when you go against God, you lose. It would be the night where my decent existence began to unravel.

It was a cold November night and I am sitting at home alone feeling the need for some companionship So I call him on his cell phone and ask, "What are you doing?" And he tells me, I'm watching television what are you doing? I'm feeling

77

lonely, and he invites me to come to his apartment to watch television with him. I drove the fifteen minutes to his place.

I had never invited him over to my home because it had been the home that I had shared with H and I did not feel comfortable bringing another man there. I parked the car in front of his apartment and I could see his apartment from outside. He lived on the first floor. It was very cold out and it been snowing for some days. I sat in the car and called him and he looked out his window and saw me, and I asked him to open the door because it was freezing outside and I didn't want to wait too long. The front door to the apartment building was locked for security reasons, to keep burglars out, is my guess. He opened the door and I immediately noticed that he was dressed appropriately this time so I thought, I am safe. We both went into the living room he sat on the chaise and I sat on the sofa. We watched television there for a little while until he asked, do you want to go to my room and watch television lying down in bed? I thought sure we both have clothes on and without a yes or a no we moved to the bedroom to watch television. We laid in bed watching television next to each other. Silly me a 51-year-old adult female with sexual desires would actually go along with this act and not expect for something to happen. But I did want something to happen. When he made the first move toward me we both ended up kissing, and then I made the next move and brought him closer to me but he was unresponsive. I looked at him and said, "I thought you desired me" and he said, he did but wanted to make sure that I desired him too. I thought that was strange. I was angry at what I had done. At that point I am not thinking about my integrity nor about morals, and I'm not feeling any shame or guilt as to what I'm about to do.

But if we confess our sins to him, he is faithful and just to forgive us our sins and to cleanse us from all wickedness. 1 John 1:9 (NLT)

SIN OVER SANCTITY

I had already made up in my mind that I was going to marry him anyway so why not. We both jumped off of the bed and I went into the bathroom to take a shower. I noticed that the bathroom was dingy-looking, paint peeling off the walls and the window sill had mildew for lack of proper cleaning. I jumped out of the shower and he grabbed a hold of me and dragged me back into the shower. We went back to the bedroom and engaged in sexual intimacy that night, and I heard a voice whisper in my ear, you are having sex with the devil. I sort of felt like it was not normal, something strange was happening to me which I had never experienced before in all my years of having sex. Whatever was there that night felt unnatural. I felt as if something or someone other than C had stepped in and taken over. What happened next was more of a surprise to me when I responded back to the voice in my head and said, I don't care! The voice that had spoken to me was not my voice but more like that of an angelic being warning me and it said, "Get away from C and stop what you are doing." I refused to listen to the voice and I blocked it out. I had neither realized how serious the offense was that I had committed nor the consequences that would affect my future and everything that I held dear to me. It was my anger talking but nevertheless, those words did come out of me.

I did the inconceivable for a Christian. I entered into the sin of fornication with this man. The voice of God had spoken to me to run, to run from him, to run away as far as possible. But instead I said to that voice on that night, "I don't care." I had really lost sight of who I was in the Kingdom of God. I had done the ungodly and Satan would put his grip on me and for the next five years, he would torment me and make my life a living hell (unbeknownst to me.)

It was evident that I was not in my right mind and I can see that it was a moment in my life where I was the most vulnerable. I had become rebellious toward my loving God without actually realizing it. Satan entered my life to create distractions and chaos all around and I had given him the opportunity to do so. I would spend the next five years fighting for my sanity. Satan and his demons were relentless. I had decided to do things my way and ignored that God knew what was best for my life. I thought that I had it all under my control. I would pray to my heavenly Father for guidance but I would still take matters into my own hands. I didn't realize that I was slowly moving away from the God who had given me a good and decent life. It only took one night of sin to change my relationship with my Living Savior, and the wonderful life I treasured.

LIVING IN SIN

In the following years, my conscience would be consumed with shame and guilt. I would be tormented day and night. Satan would continuously remind me of how I had refused to listen to the voice of God. C's presence would be a constant reminder of what I had done. I would live a life full of doubts about my relationship with God, and live in a state of confusion. I created this false life inside the real world, pretending that everything was alright that I actually ended up imprisoning myself. For a long time no one knew what I was going through during the years I was married to C nor did they know how I was feeling because I made sure that everything looked normal from the outside and it had to look that way because I was a "Christian."

God would allow certain things for Satan to do except take my life and my soul. I thank God for His mercy every day. God is so faithful and always will be faithful "to those who diligently seek Him."

CHAPTER 15

DEFIANCE

"Don't team up with those who are unbelievers. How can righteousness be a partner with wickedness? How can light live with darkness?"

1 Corinthians 6:14, NLT

GOD WARNED ME

"My marriage was doomed for failure from the very beginning because it had not been ordained by God."

This marriage, one and a half years after I widowed, was doomed for failure from the very beginning because it had not been ordained by God. I later realized that God knew that it would be a disaster and He did make several attempts to help me avoid what was coming but I did not want to listen nor did I take heed to His warnings. So, "I did it my way." I was married to someone who I did not even love or have genuine feelings for.

Because of my disobedience I would suffer one devastation after another until the end, I would not recognize myself and would loathe myself for what I had done and who I had become. During those years that I was married to C, who God had warned me against marrying, a chasm was created between my family and me. My beloved children and grandchildren later became estranged from me. If that was not enough, I lost the two properties that I had inherited through H's death. I hated my life at that time and wanted to run away. I went from a good job with a great salary, a brand new car and my own home to living in an apartment and starting from scratch. I lost it all and almost my sanity. So, I begin my story of the marriage made in hell. I went from being the happiest woman in the world, married to the man of my dreams, to being the most miserable to the point of self-loathing. I became insecure of the future and frightened about going insane during this marriage.

GOD KNOWS BEST

God knows us better than we know ourselves and he knew that being married to C would be a disaster and He wanted to help us both avoid what was coming but we moved ahead with the fake wedding that we both thought we wanted. I was the one who made the decision to marry C so there I was married to someone that I did not love and at times hated and despised. I could not stand the sight of him sometimes and I would argue with him about everything. But then, before long he showed me his fangs and his belligerent behavior was not that of a "good man" like everyone had told me he was. A good pretender is what he was. There was an ugly side to him that was scary to say the least, I was even afraid to sleep next to him at night. I can say with certainty that I understand that sex is not a priority in a good marriage but there are countless things to be considered. True love for one another should be the prerequisite.

BEING OUT OF THE WILL OF GOD

In my desperation to end the grieving over my loss, I rushed into doing things without thinking them through. For the next five years of marriage I would wander through a dense fog, unable to see what was right or wrong. I had become religious and a poor excuse for a Christian. I walked away from the will of God.

"Not everyone who says to me, 'Lord, Lord,' shall enter the kingdom of heaven, but he who does the will of my Father in heaven..."
Matthew 7:21-24 (NLT)

I was ashamed of myself and hated who I had become. I had become a phony in a 'phony marriage.' Toward my third year of marriage, I began to get more physically sick than usual with the flu and missing lots of days from work. I was also emotionally disturbed, almost losing my mind.

When I finally realized what a lie our relationship had been, three years would have passed us by. I slowly began to notice that everything I had gained the years before I met C was disappearing.

When I started writing this book, I have to admit that I was afraid to write fearing that the thoughts would continue to torment me and that I would relive those hellish years again. I lived five years in total confusion and chaos during my marriage. I call them my "hellish years." I lived in a fake marriage that had been influenced by demonic forces that I was unaware of. I pray that my story will give others hope and that they may take heed and learn from my experiences. I dare you to go with me on this hellish journey. However, I still had hope and I knew that I was not alone in this world. I knew it when I received revelation to write my story. Even when I tried to run away, as far as I could from my tormentor they followed me wherever I went because they had me in bondage and they became my constant companions. I moved away from the people I loved the most and I missed them tremendously and how I ached to be with them again.

CHAPTER 16

VICTIM

"Stay alert! Watch out for your great enemy, the devil. He prowls around like a roaring lion, looking for someone to devour." 1 Peter 5:8, NLT

SATAN THE MARIONETTIST

"Satan knows your worst fears."

I have shared how I met C and how I married him only after knowing him for six months. I really did not feel any love for him nor did I ever believe that he was the right man. So how was it that I found myself drawn to him and went along with the dating and the courtship? I was like a puppet on a string and little did I know that Satan himself was the marionettist pulling the strings. I was unaware, of course that he had been orchestrating the entire scenario and that I would end up married to a man I did not love. There was no real romance between us. I would eventually end up loathing him and wanting him gone.

I thought the only way to escape from him was that he would divorce me or commit adultery so that I would have a reason to leave him. That kind of thinking was not "Christ-like" but that goes to show what kind of a mindset I was in. It was awful when I think about it. Since we had decided to get married, why not have sex, right! No, wrong! Why did I not run away and cancel the wedding? I asked myself that question many times.

I thought I had the license to sin just because he would be my husband in a few months. During my marriage, I would suffer the consequences of my actions. I became so ashamed of myself I just wanted to die. I also felt that I was going insane. During my third year of marriage, I thought of committing suicide on two separate occasions by swallowing pills. Sometimes I would envision myself in a mental ward, in one of the inpatient units I worked overtime in but God was keeping me regardless of my disobedience.

SATAN THE TORMENTOR

I had unleashed Satan through my rebellious actions. I was tormented by the devil and his demons for five years in my home, (they specifically occupied my bedroom but followed me around the house just to scare me to death.) Satan knows your worse fears. Those were the most awful and most difficult years of my life.

Satan had me all confused and lost and I felt stuck in my marriage. It was not that I could not get out of the marriage because I did not have the means, but it was the cloud of confusion that Satan had put over me that I could not see the way to get free. I had money, a car, and several properties that I could have moved into. The more I fought to free myself of Satan the more I saw myself sucked in by him. I dreaded going to sleep at night because I knew that I would spend most of the night rebuking him and his demons from my room. I would pray and read the Bible before going to sleep at night but I could still sense them around me. They sensed that I was easily scared and they knew that I feared them, and so they would feed on that fear. The presence of evil was strong and I'd see dark shadows lurking around in the room or feel them standing behind me or making noise so I'd know they were there. They would only leave me alone, for a little while when I would cry out to God to "help me!"

MARRIAGE ARRANGED IN HELL

Marrying outside of God's will would be the beginning of a marriage made in hell and I would live in that hell for five years and regret every waking moment of it. Meeting C was no coincidence as I would later find out the truth. He was just as much the victim of Satan's plan as I was.

Satan wanted to destroy God's plan and purpose for my life. Satan knew that C was the perfect candidate for his scheme. I was God's child and even I knew what God was preparing me for, a great calling. Satan knew that he had to stop whatever it was God had called me for and he would use whatever means he could to do so. It was the most deceiving plan that the devil could ever had devised against me. To throw me into a whirlwind of sin, shame, guilt, and deception.

I WAS SATAN'S INTENDED VICTIM

I, unfortunately, did not come to this realization until some years into my marriage. In my human and finite mind, I thought that I had solely created the mess in my life (not knowing that I was Satan's intended victim). Oh yes I definitely had something to do with the choices that I had made. But I asked myself how could I a Christian woman get myself to a point in my life where I am contemplating suicide and not just once but on two separate occasions. I did not know who I was and so I began to loathe myself and my life, and that was definitely not "Christ-like." I found myself in a desperate situation and could not see a way out of the mess that I had created, all because I did not take heed to God's warnings. I wanted to believe that this mess was not entirely my fault but that marrying him was what had cursed me and caused a "domino affect" in my life where I would begin to lose everything that I had inherited and had owned, even my new ventures. But it was more than a mess, it was a disaster. As if a hurricane had hit my life and everything like my joy, peace, stability, finances, family, and health went everywhere like flying debris.

CHAPTER 17

SOVEREIGN GOD

"Stay alert! Watch out for your great enemy, the devil. He prowls around like a roaring lion, looking for someone to devour." 1 Peter 5:8 (NLT)

GOD IS TRUE

"I gave the enemy power and the strength he needed to control me"

I gave the enemy power and the strength he needed to control me but I did not know this back then. When I began to seek for things that fed my desires and were not fitting for the kingdom of God I gave Satan a foothold. The mistake that I made was to think that Satan couldn't come against me as long as I believed in God. As you continue to journey with me you will see how easy it was for Satan to have invaded my life. He will try every angle he can to get to those that serve God the most. The Bible tells us that Satan was an angel of the Lord in heaven and his name was Lucifer but he rebelled against God because he wanted to be "just like God." God is the only true and sovereign God. He threw Satan out of heaven along with the angels that followed him.

"How you are fallen from heaven, O shining star, son of the morning! You have been thrown down to the earth, you who destroyed the nations of the world. For you said to yourself, I will ascend to heaven and set my throne above God's stars. I will preside on the mountain of the gods far away in the north. I will climb to the highest heavens and be like the Most High."
Isaiah 14:12-14 (NLT)

Satan is the great deceiver and is always looking to deceive anyone that opens the door to him. I was not vigilant and I took my eyes from God. Satan is forever looking for whom he can devour and manipulate into serving him.

GOD OPENS YOUR SPIRITUAL EYES

I do believe that I was under a dumb cloud because everything that I had learned during the seventeen years since my salvation, my attendance in church Sunday after Sunday and all the Bible study classes I took on Wednesdays, became a total fog to me. Even as I continued to attend church and knew the scriptures about evil spirits and how to pray them out it just was not working for me. I would eventually know why none of my prayers and going to church was working for me. It was not until I saw through my spiritual eyes what God wanted me to see that I was able to finally rid myself from Satan and his demons. I was in spiritual blindness but eventually my eyes were opened and I soon saw the deception that had been orchestrated by Satan to pull me away from God's kingdom.

GOD KNOWS SATAN IS RELENTLESS

Fortunately for me, there is nothing that Satan does that God is not aware of and allows. I was the victim of his deception when I refused to listen to the voice of God. I was deep in sin when God attempted to rescue me but I told God "I don't care." I knew very well that I was fornicating but I did not think that it would cost me what it did. I desired to be loved by someone and so I took him since he was available and he wanted me as well. I threw myself at him without reservation and without thinking about the consequences of that choice. What would follow next after I made that decision would turn my entire life and that of my family into a whirlwind. My actions and disobedience to the voice of God would cause me not forgiving myself for years because I was not worthy.

I thought that because I was a Christian and had been attending church for seventeen years that I knew how to handle evil spirits and their attacks but what I did not realize back then was that I had to be totally sold out to the Holy One to have that kind of power. For my prayers to have been effective when the attacks of the devil came against me, I needed to have been prepared and armed with the Holy Spirit and prepared to hear the voice of God when He speaks. I now know that I have always been a target of the devil. That he had tried on many occasions to destroy me only I did not know it then. Satan's attempts against me began a long time ago when I was a child. My understanding of what I have heard, through the many preachers that I have heard preach is that Satan does not know your future but he does know your past and your present state. Satan is relentless.

CHAPTER 18

THE PAST

"This means that anyone who belongs to Christ has become a new person. The old life is gone; a new life has begun!" 2 Corinthians 5:17(NLT)

BORN INTO SIN

As I started to write my story it all began to make sense to me that although I had been saved from my old life for many years how was it that I reverted to my old sinful nature. It became apparent to me that I had never really given up on my old life but that I had stored it away instead of burying it for good. There were things in my life that I just assume leave alone but the memories however horrible, they would always appear in my thoughts to remind me of what a terrible life I lived prior to my conversion. When I gave my life to Christ and began to attend church and seek God for myself, there had to be an overall transformation of my thinking, behavior, and attitude. I should never try to justify my sin of disobedience to the law of God because I was made new by the blood of Jesus, my Savior.

GENERATIONAL CURSES

I grew up around my mother's family who practiced all sorts of voodoo and witchcraft. Growing up around my aunts never surprised me as to what the conversation would be about. Discussions about sorcery, black magic and spiritualism were always routinely around my maternal family. It was never a boring or dull moment whenever they would get together with mom. I was raised in an environment that it was normal to mix religion with the occult and they did not think to see the difference between the two. In my culture, believing in the occult and in the dead spirits having special powers to heal or to take a person's soul from them was as normal as breathing. I'd sit around my aunts and listen to them talk about the time that a woman they knew had been "jinxed" and ended up falling down the stairs and breaking her neck. I heard them talking about this beautiful woman that my aunts knew and she lived in a two story house with her family. They said that one day this woman was standing at the top of the stairs looking into a mirror that was in the middle of the top landing and that when she looked into the mirror she saw an ugly creature staring back at her and the shock threw her back and she fell down the stairs. They mentioned that someone had envied her and wanted her out of the way, and so she was scared to death was the rumor.

I never practiced "voodoo" or "witchcraft" to hurt anyone but I had attended some "spiritualist centers" in my young adult days to have my palm read and to buy a few bottles of potions that the Palm reader would sell and tell me that I needed it to ward off evil spirits that were trying to harm me, yeah right! I did not know the truth about what it meant to go into those places nor the impact that it would have on my soul later in life. I had grown up believing that it was alright to visit those places. I was told that it did more good than harm when you went to visit a place like that so I did as I observed my mom's family members do.

My mom did not care about going to those places but I know she knew when a bad spirit was in the home. My mom would sense an evil spirit and she would start shaking uncontrollably and swinging her arms all over the place saying things like "they have done it again" and then she would drop to the floor and wiggle around like a serpent until it was all over, whatever it was. It was almost like a ritual she had to perform to stop what evil spirit had attached itself to her. Watching my mom and her family do those kinds of things had me living in fear for a long time. I have to admit that when I became a Christian it took me a long time before I could feel comfortable sleeping with the lights completely off. I would have a night light on all night. I believe that I had never gotten over the fears inflicted on me by family beliefs and rituals. Generational curses had not been broken and so there were evil spirits always lurking nearby.

SATAN IS REAL

I did not know what I know now that evil spirit cannot harm me. They can try to scare me to death if I let them, and I now know that I give the demons the power when I am fearful. Another lesson to keep in mind is that Satan does not come to you looking like a disfigured monster with horns coming out of his head with a long black beard and wearing a red cape. He comes disguised like a normal human. He comes to you when you are most vulnerable and have dropped your shields. I cannot speak for others in the faith or anyone else for that matter but regarding what I went through I can only speak for myself about how I experienced what I experienced and I must say, Satan is real.

Simon, Simon, Satan has asked to sift each of you like wheat. But I have pleaded in prayer for you, Simon, that your faith should not fail."

Luke 22:31 (NLT)

CHAPTER 19

UNWISE DECISION

"The woman was convinced. She saw that the tree was beautiful and its fruit looked delicious, and she wanted the wisdom it would give her. So she took some of the fruit and ate it. Then she gave some to her husband, who was with her, and he ate it, too." Genesis 3:6 (NLT)

MARRIAGE PROPOSAL

One evening in November, C invites me out to dinner at a restaurant called the Mona Lisa, (my close friends and family called me Mona). I dressed up for the occasion in a pair of gold/winter white slacks and a winter white sweater with a pair of winter white boots; and a winter white short imitation fur jacket. I met him at his apartment. He had on a black turtleneck sweater and black slacks with his black leather jacket, and he looked quite handsome. I drove us to the restaurant in my brand new 2004 Saturn.

The restaurant is on the outskirts of the city in a quaint town called Newtown. It is my first time going to this restaurant and I'm impressed with the place. We entered into a foyer where the lights have been brought down low and it's quite romantic. I'm now in the dining area and the room is full of couples talking privately to one another. There are white linen tables with candles lit in the center. Crystal wine glasses beautifully placed on top. There is music playing in the background. I don't see the musician. I met his younger brother, (from a different mother) for the first and I also met his girlfriend for the first time. They had been waiting for us at the place's parking lot. After the introductions, we order dinner. I'm not sure what I ordered.

I think we had been sitting there for about half an hour when he pulls out a small black velvet box and gives it to me. I get so excited because the moment has come for the proposal for marriage. I open the box and in it is the most beautiful engagement ring. It has many diamonds clustered together on the sides and one big one on the top. In the excitement of it all, I start to hyperventilate and had to leave the table and run to the restroom and the girlfriend follows behind me. I was not hyperventilating because of overwhelming joy, instead it was because of the doubts about my future with someone I wasn't sure I had real feelings for. I think that I was looking to secure my future, I wasn't getting any younger. When I eventually calmed down I went back to the table and as soon as I sat down C asked me, "Would you marry me?" I said yes and we kissed. I admit it was a wonderful surprise, and I had a good time with the company.

His brother and girlfriend offered to pay for the entire dinner, and that was very nice of them. I really had no idea that he would propose so soon. I guess it was the discussion we had about not having sex until that ring was around my finger. I should have said until we were married.

HAVING SECOND THOUGHTS

Instead of taking him back to his apartment, we went to a hotel. His kids were staying in the apartment that night. We decided not to stay out all night. In the hotel room, I noticed something strange about his left foot that made me freak out but I did not let him see my face as I looked at it. I gasped and my eyes opened wide. I was so scared. I thought, I'm going to hell tonight this devil is going to kill me. He is the child of the devil. My first instinct was to run out of that room as fast as I could and not look back. I though, so this is what God had tried to warn me about. But I decided to brave it out and then I thought, you watch too many demon possess movies. I was creeping myself out so I decided to ask him about it. He told me that he was born with a deformity. I believed it. I felt sorry for him at that moment but at the same time I wanted to give him back the engagement ring and run out of that hotel room and never see him again. I really did think that he was a demon. But again that inner voice said to me humble yourself, stop thinking you are better than him. That lying demon kept me from running away. That was my chance to get away clean.

WHO ARE YOU LISTENING TO?

Back when the voice had tried to stop me from having relations with C, I did not really know whose voice I was listening to. I do know that I really did not want to marry him but that voice kept right on telling me to humble myself, I listened to it. I was so confused. I don't know what I was doing with him. I was not even in love with him. I just know that he was there and I clung to him. For what I don't know. I really didn't need him because I had plenty of money; property and a good paying job.

The strangest thing of it all is that I wasn't feeling any guilt about my behavior. I had refused to accept responsibility for going against my better judgment. I rebelled against my own moral principles. I did not know what in the world I was doing and why I was doing it. Whatever it was that was driving me to do the things I was doing, I was defenseless to control it. I was being led by a force that was driving my desires to be with someone even if it was someone that I had no real true feelings for. On our honeymoon I would get a glimpse of what a serious mistake I had made and my life would never be the same.

CHAPTER 20

THE PEARLS

"Teacher," they said to Jesus, "this woman was caught in the act of adultery. The law of Moses says to stone her. What do you say?" They were trying to trap him into saying something they could use against him, but Jesus stooped down and wrote in the dust with his finger. They kept demanding an answer, so he stood up again and said, all right, but let the one who has never sinned throw the first stone!" Then he stooped down again and wrote in the dust. When the accusers heard this, they slipped away one by one, beginning with the oldest, until only Jesus was left in the middle of the crowd with the woman. Then Jesus stood up again and said to the woman, "Where are your accusers? Didn't even one of them condemn you?" "No, Lord," she said. And Jesus said, "Neither do I. Go and sin no more." John 8:1-11 (NLT)

TRUE CONVICTION

So, I am engaged and picking out a date for the wedding. I can't remember why we picked the month of March except that it would be three months from the time he proposed to me on that cold night on November 17th.

We continued to engage in sexual intimacy during the month of November and into the month of December. But on one night in December, something happened to me while we were being intimate, and it was at that moment I realized what a sinner I had been. I felt so convicted, ashamed, and dirty. I saw a vision of myself lying in a filthy gutter with garbage all around me reaching out my hand to the first male that walked by me. I heard myself say: you are dirty, used, and abused. That night I cried myself to sleep thinking I'm lying next to a nobody, and felt like he was a John that I had just picked up in the street somewhere. I allowed him into my decent life, (not that he was a bad person because he wasn't and he took very good care of himself and he was no bum.) I knew that this was not a good way to feel even though I was about to marry him, it just didn't feel right. Years later my spirit would reveal to me that I "had given my pearls to the pigs."

"Don't give what is holy to dogs or throw your pearls to pigs. Otherwise, they will trample them and then tear you to pieces."

Matthew 7:6-8 (NLT)

I didn't know what to do and I didn't have anyone to talk to about what I was going through. I was really feeling alone and wanted so much to have a companion but that wasn't the way of going about it.

STOP SINNING

I woke up the next morning and I rushed out apartment crying all the way home. Then, I felt the urge to call the Pastor of my Church and I told him that I had slept with C and that I was feeling horrible about it, and felt guilty that I had done something very wrong in the eyes of God. I didn't know what to do and I needed to repent. At that moment, all I wanted was for the earth to swallow me up. I asked him, should I go to the elders of the church and tell them what I have done? I thought it was something I was supposed to do. The Pastor told me, say nothing to anyone, you have done the right thing by calling me and you should not do it again.

IT'S YOUR SIN

I am reminded of what Jesus Christ did when Mary Magdalena was brought to him by the Jewish leaders, who had caught her in the act of adultery. Jesus returned to the Mount of Olives, but early the next morning he was back at the Temple. A crowd soon gathered, and he sat down and taught them. As he was speaking, the teachers of religious law and the Pharisees brought a woman who had been caught in the act of adultery. They put her in front of the crowd.

My Pastor said, acknowledging that you have sinned and feeling convicted is a good thing. I thanked him and went home and asked God to forgive me for all my transgressions against Him and for all of my iniquities. I also promised God that I would not have sexual intimacy with him until we got married and I kept my promise and we did not have sex until the night of our wedding, three months later.

DEATH FOLLOWS SIN
(a prelude to what's to come later)

I had gotten accustomed to being around him and I visited him often. On this one particular night, something strange happened. It was towards the very end of December and it had started to snow very heavy outside. I stayed the night so as not to take the risk of having an accident while driving home. I chose to sleep on the living room sofa. That night I had a dream that a skinny looking young teenager about seventeen years old with medium dark complexion, dark brown hair and eyes had put a pair of house sleepers at the end of his bed, but instead of it being the bed it was the sofa where I was sleeping. I became frightened because it appeared so real that I woke up screaming for C. I asked him if I could join him in bed and I ran out of the living room as fast as I could and jumped into bed, I was really scared. We both kept the promise and did not engage in sexual intimacy.

The next morning as C was making coffee, I start telling him all about my dream, I said, the young man stared at me so intently with a serious look on his face before he started walking slowly down toward my feet and placing the slippers that he had in his hands at the foot of the sofa where I was sleeping, and I'm up on my right elbow looking at him moving about and then he disappeared as soon as he appeared. I was so spooked that's why I screamed your name out and asked to come to your bed.

I thought to myself that this boy was trying to tell me something about C, but I didn't share that with him. I'm not sure if he was paying me any attention or was more involved in making his coffee because he did not appear moved by my story. Instead he had a blank stare on his face which made me think that he did not find my dream strange at all or he wasn't listening to me.

I became curious to know what had happened to that young boy. I thought that maybe he knew something about this young boy's death and did not want to talk about it. But sometime later that morning when we're sitting down at the table having the coffee he told me the story of the young boy I had described to him. It was his younger brother who when he was sixteen years old drowned in their uncle's pool. He said, we had been playing in the pool for some time and my uncle and I were hungry and we got out to get something to eat and when I returned to the pool he was floating in the pool dead. I don't know what happened he said. He continued to share that, when my brother died my mom threw away all of his photos and asked every family member to throw away every photo they had of him. He was to be forgotten forever and never to be mentioned again. The pain was too great for my mom to bear.

I felt that I had stirred up something in him that he would rather not remember and he appeared saddened by having told me the story. The death of a dear one is so unbearable that we try to bury our memories of them as they are buried in the ground.

CHAPTER 21

MORE WARNING SIGNS

Oh, foolish Galatians! Who has cast an evil spell on you? For the meaning of Jesus Christ's death was made as clear to you as if you had seen a picture of his death on the cross...After starting your new lives in the Spirit, why are you now trying to become perfect by your own human effort? Galatians 3:1-3 (NLT)

TWO PASTORS, PLEASE

In January of 2005 I decided to speak with my Pastor and ask him to marry us. But C wanted his Pastor to marry us and I wanted my Pastor to marry us. Right there I should have picked up on how our marriage was going to turn out. It was another sign and I didn't see it. So, he made an appointment with his pastor and I made an appointment with my pastor. I wanted my Pastor because I had been going to my church for nine years when he had only started going to his a few months after we had met. He claimed that he had been going to church before we met on a sporadic basis to bring his youngest daughter.

WHAT'S WRONG WITH THIS PICTURE?

I should have realized that something was very wrong with this picture but I ignored my inner voice warning me, instead I would listen to the other voice, (the bad one.)

He had told me that he grew up in a Pentecostal church but stopped attending church at the age of twelve and would attend his church of choice only on a sporadic basis. I had told him about my intentions never to go out with or marry an unbeliever and I told him that on our first date. I was adamant about not marrying someone who didn't love God and didn't go to church. However, I did notice that he started to attend church regularly so I was content with that, and I thought that if he was willing to go to church and be baptized, then that was alright with me.

Anyway, we both made the appointments and we started the marriage counseling classes and we set the date with our Pastors to marry us in my church and both Pastors agreed to our plans. We received marriage counseling from our Pastors but I sense that both Pastors were somewhat uncertain about our marriage and during their lecture to us they made it obvious. I could be assuming something that is not there but when his Pastor asked us, are you sure you're not rushing into this marriage? I assumed that he meant that we were prematurely setting the wedding date without taking the time to know more about each other. I also thought since we were adults, they couldn't say much about it, and that we were going to get married regardless of their opinions. That was a terrible thing to think but I had already had sex with C and to me getting married was a way of getting things right with God and my conscience would be clean, silly me.

DON'T SHUN WISDOM

I thought that I had everything under control, ha! That was a laugh. I was becoming more of a fool and didn't see it coming because I thought that I was mature enough and I was supposed to know everything, yeah right. So, we scheduled appointments to meet with both Pastors. We met with his Pastor first. His Pastor wanted to know, why are you both desiring to get married, and what are your children's thoughts about this. Have you both talked about any financial issues and concerns. He shared his spiritual point of view with us, and discussed all that a marriage entails and what married couples are to mean to each other. We both told him, we have fallen in love, and then I said, I really don't care for the dating factor, I want to get married. Did I say that I had fallen in love with him? I did say it but did I really mean it? The Pastor knew that we had only known each other a few months. He had asked us before, how long have you been dating each other? He looked at us strange and I caught that look but I am not sure that C did. I could notice a smirk on his face, but I let it go and didn't say anything to C about it. When I think about it his Pastor never did give us his blessing. I think he knew something that I didn't but wouldn't say anything because we did not give him the opportunity.

Then we went to see my Pastor and he spoke to me first while his son, who was the youth minister at the time, had a private conversation with C. My Pastor then met with us together and directed his questions to C, "are you aware of the aspect of what taking care of a family is about? You will have financial responsibilities." C told both Pastors that he would care of seventy-five percent of the household expenses, and I would not have to worry about anything that he would take care of his share. He assured my Pastor that he had everything under control. My Pastor knew that I had only widowed a year before and he did not want anyone taking advantage of me. Both Pastor and son gave me their blessings to marry him.

WHAT DID YOU LEARN?

So there we were attending the marriage classes arranged by my Pastor and we met once a week with the co-pastor of my church to discuss the material that he had given to us to read about marriage.

We'd get together in the evenings and go through the book that the co-pastor had handed us. We would ask each other questions about it. Most of the time I was the only one reading this book I'd ask him questions about what I had just read to him. Sometimes we'd read it together. Most of the questions dealt with what the marriage meant, what was the responsibility of each one of us as we joined in holy matrimony. There were questions about our likes and dislikes and about family conflicts and about finances. He always had a positive answer to give and it helped built my confidence more in him.

I was learning more about him through that book. I thought no one is that perfect, there has to be some flaws in each of us. The book was enlightening and it was a good experience for me. I began to understand what a true relationship should be like before marriage. I enjoyed those nights and I never thought about breaking my promise. I was determined to wait to say I do at the altar in front of God, along with our friends and family members.

TWO DEAD PEOPLE

"For the wages of sin is death..." (Romans 6:23, NLT)

However, during this waiting, I started to notice some-thing strange about me and my feelings toward him. Whenever, I got close to him to show him affection, I felt like I was embracing a corpse, he was very unresponsive. Most times I'd think maybe he would be tired from work or would have a million things on his mind. I guess for the most part I was looking for some kind of assurance that we both really did want to get married. He would come toward me and grab me in his arms but I could not feel the warm fuzzy love in my heart, only numbness. There was never any true affectionate warmth between the two of us and I couldn't figure out why we even bothered to get married. I say we had a dead marriage. We were like two dead people going through the motions.

I thought maybe he would change and I could teach him how to be passionate, but it never happened. Sorry to have to say it so bluntly. Yeah, I knew that something was starting off wrong with this relationship, so why did I stay in this God forsaken relationship? It was that inner voice in me telling me things like, he is a "good man" and you can be his help mate.

I guess I wasn't as mature of a Christian as I thought. At that moment in my life at fifty-one years old, I was lost, and confused. God should had been my only refuge when I was feeling lonely. He would have made a way if only I had waited. God will talk to us and let his presence be felt.

CHAPTER 22

WHAT A MESS...

So I say to those who aren't married and to widows—it's better to stay unmarried, just as I am. ⁹ But if they can't control themselves, they should go ahead and marry. It's better to marry than to burn with lust.

1 Corinthians 7:8-9 (NLT)

WHERE ARE MY FUNDS?

Lack of affection wasn't the only oddity in this marriage, and I would later discover other strange discrepancies and happenings throughout my six-year marriage.

The preparations are underway and we start planning for our wedding day. I sit with him to discuss the expenses, and where were we going to have the reception; and all about who would attend our wedding and who was going to be in our wedding party. We both decided that our children should all be part of the wedding party and that his cousin would be the best man and my daughter would be the maid of honor.

I mentioned the place where my niece had her bridal shower a year before and that it was a perfect location, spacious enough to accommodate about 125 guests and it's a fairly nice restaurant/banquet hall in Monroe Connecticut.

I called to make an appointment to discuss the rental cost, food, and other amenities. He met me there and I spoke to the person in charge of the hall and she gave us a reasonable price per plate and she told us, we will take care of all the decorations as long as you bring them on time the day of the wedding. I had to leave a deposit to hold the hall for that date and I signed the agreement. He had no money so I wrote out a check and gave it to her as a retainer. I had already spent money to pay a month's security and a month's rent for our new apartment. It was in a better neighborhood than the one he was living at so that we can move into it once we got married. Because there was no way I would be moving into his small and dingy apartment and I definitely was not bringing him to the home that I had shared with my late husband. He agreed that he would pay the remaining balance as soon as he had the money, and he already owed me part of the rent money for our new apartment. My savings were slowly disappearing, and there I thought that I was marrying someone with plenty of money that would take care of me and my family for life. It was obvious that none of this was making sense so why did I continue to move ahead. I was not in control. I felt that I had no one to turn to for advice. "I had made my bed and had to lie in it." I was beginning to feel ashamed of myself as to what I had gotten myself into and with whom. What a mess!

So the remaining balance for the hall was paid for by C. I ordered the cake that the best man paid for it. The cake was a beautiful three tier cake made white frosting and yellow flowers around each tier and green leaves that cascaded from the top tier to the bottom tier of the cake. I had spent money on buying all the girls their outfits including dresses to shoes to hair accessories and jewelry. C had to rent his tuxedos and for both his sons.

YOU MADE YOUR BED, LIE IN IT...

That was only the beginning of all the mess I would find myself in. If someone had told me what a mess I was going to get myself into I never would have believed them. Although his second ex-wife did try to tell me the mess I was getting myself into, she waited only one week before our wedding day to tell me. She told that if I was looking for just companionship then he was the man but not to expect anything else out of him nor from him. I was expecting to be rescued and secure, what a fool I was to believe that foolish nonsense.

Here again is a warning sign that I did not take heed of as the inner voice kept reminding that he was a "good man" and that these two women were foolish to leave him. I was about to get married in one week and had already spent every cent I had left from the insurance money to pay for the apartment and the wedding, as well as the shop which still needed more material to completed the work.

I kept going deeper and deeper into a spiral of a mess and the absurdity of it is that I was doing it with my eyes wide open. I was the chief operator of the train that was headed for a wreck. I had been spending toward a wedding that I was not anointed to participate in because God had already told me that he was not the man that I should marrying. But in my rebelliousness I forged ahead in that speeding locomotive that would leave many hurting and scarred for life. Nothing will ever be the same.

WEDDING DAY...

On the day of the wedding, I was still hesitant about marrying C that I called my friend, who is a real estate lawyer, and asked him if I could sign a prenuptial agreement. C was somewhat offended by that gesture but I had to make sure that he was not marrying me for my material possessions. I return to our new apartment to get ready for the four o'clock wedding at my church. Yes, we both settled on my church for the ceremony. In the meantime, he is at his cousin's place getting ready with the guys.

The males wore black tuxedos, the bridegroom wore an ivory color jacket and so did the best man; and they both had yellow flowers in their lapels. I'm having my hair and make-up done by his brother's girlfriend, who is a make-up artist. She had also done the girls hair and make-up. My daughter and granddaughters and C' girls wore yellow dresses with silver high heel sandals and their hairs were up in buns with baby breaths around the bun. So far everything was running on schedule. I even had time to take pictures with the girls after we were all dressed up. I drive myself to the church and my daughter drives her car with the girls there. I remember two things about the church ceremony, one was turning around after I said "I do" to C and saying to everyone I did it!

I don't know why that was so important. Like why did I have to say that. The other thing that I remember was running out of the church and going into the shiny black truck (he had purchased several months before) with my beautiful off-white silk wedding dress and satin off-white shoes

The hall was beautifully decorated in white linen table cloths and yellow flowers. Souvenirs adorned each table, and there was crystal glassware and shiny flatware on the tables. My stepson asked a friend/church member to be the DJ and he drove from Hartford with his wife to play both Christian and secular music and didn't charge us.

BE SET FREE...

Don't team up with those who are unbelievers. How can righteousness be a partner with wickedness? How can light live with darkness?

2 Corinthians 6:14 (NLT)

The theme I decided on was "let the sun shine down" since the decorations around in the hall were mostly in yellow. I wanted to give the place a warm feeling like that of the sun shining in the hall from the outside. I so wanted to give God honor for this day that I asked a couple of my church sisters to minister a praise dance at my wedding. They ushered in the spirit in that hall that I felt a presence of peace and harmony in the place. I did not get the whole picture back then of how I would spend the following years in a dark place begging to be set free.

Prior to this day I had been struggling with my own personal family issues around my marriage to C which caused conflict with my son who was away in California on a military base and he was very upset with me and didn't want to talk to me. My daughter couldn't figure out what I was doing and I could tell she wasn't in agreement to be part of the wedding; and my granddaughters were somewhat sad and acting out. They all appeared to be very distant from me when at one time we were all very close. I began to think that once this wedding day was over and done with that everything would return to normal.

C had to deal with some conflict of his own with one of his ex-wives because she didn't want their children to be in the wedding. She was the one who called my work a week before. But the children rebelled against her told her that they were going to be in their father's wedding. My granddaughters cried at my wedding because they didn't want me marrying someone else since I had been grandpa's wife. My daughter felt the same way and she had made the comment to one of my relatives that I was her dad's wife. I was told this story a few years later by my cousin who was a guest at my wedding.

NEITHER ONE OF US KNEW THE TRUTH...

C still believed that this wedding was God ordained. I tried telling him four years into our marriage the truth with tears in my eyes and asking him to forgive me but he refused to believe me. I told him the truth about me being rebellious toward God and how God had told me not to marry him. C still talks about what a wonderful day it was for him and how the guests had complimented him and said things like, what a beautiful couple we made and how we both looked to be so in love, and how happy we both looked. That our wedding was a beautiful wedding. He'd say things like, how great everything turned out and how the guests had a good time at our wedding. I wanted to be just as enthusiastic but I couldn't.

CHAPTER 23

CAN THIS REALLY BE HAPPENING?

And what do you benefit if you gain the whole world but lose your own soul? Is anything worth more than your soul? Matthew 16:26 (NLT)

THE RESORT

When we got home from the wedding reception, we went to the living room, he sat on the floor and I was on the sofa opposite him. I took out all of the wedding gift cards that our friends and family had given to us and I counted close to four thousand dollars and he looked at me and asked me, where is my share of the money? I looked at him and said, I can't keep this money. I have to pay it back to the bank since I had borrowed from the bank to pay for our wedding and for our honeymoon trip. You see I had to borrow money from my bank so that I wouldn't go into my credit union savings account that I kept as an emergency fund. I figured that I would pay the bank back with the gift money. He seemed disappointed but so was I that I had to borrow the money in the first place to pay for our wedding.

I was definitely not liking what I was experiencing on my wedding night, as a matter of fact, I was feeling very foolish and thinking this is not right and what is happening? I was not in my right mind when I made the decision to get married. I understand now that I was in no condition to make sound decisions because I had to have been emotionally weak to know what I was doing never mind in what I was getting myself into.

But there I was married and starting a new marriage without funds.

But, he had the solution and I held him up to it since he had told both his Pastor and my Pastor that he would carry seventy-five percent of the expenses in the household. The honeymoon trip had been paid in advance and he had his credit cards as I had mine and we went onto this island, that I swore I would never go back to if I can help it. The honeymoon night was not what I expected and I was left dissatisfied the entire week we were there. In other words, there was no "love lost" between us. The honeymoon period was over before it got started. I had been feeling this loss of connection between us even prior to the day of the wedding. The island resort was extremely beautiful in comparison to others I had been to in the past.

The hotel gave us a beautiful suite with stairs that lead to the bedroom, a huge living room and an immense bathroom with a Jacuzzi tub, that we never shared together. There were palm trees and exotic plants everywhere. I had all the tropical fruits I wanted the entire day long. I'd have a light breakfast, a delicious lunch from the buffet and a sit-in dinner at night of steak one night, lobster the other with all the side dishes available. I was there to enjoy myself and eat until my heart's desire. I'd spend most of the day in the swimming pool and soaking in the sunshine beaming down on us every day, and then at night I'd go to their nightclub dancing and for karaoke music. I like to sing. I wore all the beautiful summer outfits that I had taken with me and took plenty of photos of myself. I realized one thing while I was there that I could substitute intimate affection for things that made me feel happy and better about myself. I was determined to enjoy my life no matter the painful situations I found myself in and he would have to keep up with me or leave.

THE SCHOOL

When I got home after our honeymoon we both went back to work. I continued to attend my own church and he went to his. I also went back to school to complete the vision/mission God had for me. I had seen the vision of great and mighty things that were about to come my way and I knew in my heart that it was but the grace of God who had made it all come to fruition, and I was as happy as happy can get.

The school itself had a good reputation for having the best Masters' program in Social Work studies and I was very fortunate to have attended that school. The day that I first entered that school to register for my courses it's as if my life had a new meaning and that wonderful things were going to come out of it. At first, I felt that my life was over when H died. I had to realize that God had plans for me. So I knew what I had to do for God so I could move ahead. I had been admitted that being accepted into the Master's program was God's divine appointment. I chose to be obedient and go ahead and get that degree but I had started to hate going to the school because I'd cry every time I drove to it. My heart would hurt again remembering that H had attended the school several years earlier and received his Bachelors' degree in Business Administration. I'd leave the building and the memory of him would bring a flood of tears to my eyes and many days I'd cry all the way home. I would scream loud in my car that if someone were to see me they would think I was going mad in the car. I would mainly slam my hands on the steering wheel, good thing the airbag never deployed, and I would scream at God until I would feel a calming presence and I would calm down. I'd still be whimpering all the way home. I could not wait for the day that I would graduate from that school so that I would never have to see it ever again. I was doing what I had to do and decided that nothing was going to spoil it for me.

THE NEW APARTMENT

I am married and living in my new apartment, paying more rent than I was in my home, which within a few months the mortgage would be paid for but I would not be living there to enjoy that benefit. However, I was believing that someday C would buy us a new home. I was looking forward to a life of wealth. When we had decided to get married, we looked around for a decent apartment, in a good neighborhood in Bridgeport that bordered Fairfield and Trumbull Ct. Many places were too expensive or the wait for a vacancy was too long than we were willing to wait for an apartment and we were getting frustrated looking. Well, one day he mentioned to me, my aunt C told me to check this apartment that she had gone to see for herself but decided not to take, so maybe you and I can go see today. It appeared that she had been looking at a few apartments herself because she was between houses, selling one and buying another. I went with him to see the apartment and I liked everything about it. It was convenient for the time being. I decided to sign a one-year lease. I liked it was big enough for the two of us. It was cozy and I like cozy. It had the modern look with its winter white wall to wall carpeting, and spacious bedrooms and brand new kitchen cabinets. It was close to the shopping mall and one of my girlfriends who happened to own a home around the corner from me. The neighborhood that bordered Trumbull and Fairfield was quiet and clean and that was important to me as well. For the most part the neighbors kept pretty much to themselves and they were polite when they saw me come into the building. In the beginning of my move to the new apartment the neighbors reminded me of people out of a Norman Rockwell painting.

The nearby university used these apartments as dorms for some of their students. I knew that the students were there only during the end of a semester year and summer because they would have their going back home parties and for the most part they were loud.

His children started coming over every weekend which started to conflict with my school work time. I had to study for school assignments and work on my research paper. I treasured alone time and also wanted time with their dad, since we were married! I had been married less than a year when I wanted out of the marriage but I needed somewhere to live before I made the move. I thought about moving back to my old home in Stratford since it was still my home, until the unexpected happened which I had not foreseen.

LOST PROPERTY... LOST MEMORIES

I made the decision to rent my duplex where I lived with H for all those years since it was going to be vacated by me. I thought rent it out and make some money from it. At the time and I asked C to help find someone. I wanted to rent it to someone trustworthy, respectable, and who would keep it clean. I also had to be careful who would rent the upstairs floor because the downstairs was being rented by my ex-brother in-law's ex-girlfriend and her two young children, boys. C mentioned that a good friend of his was looking for an apartment and that I could trust this person. He told me, you can trust him because I know him. He has his own home security alarm company, and is respectable and clean. I Trusted C's judgment about this guy and agreed to meet with him. My problem was solved so I thought. I met with this friend at our apartment and he told me that had a teenage son who would be moving in with him. He was a burly guy about 6'2', unattractive and spoke in a low rough voice. I wouldn't want to run into him a dark alley, I'd be scared he'd hurt me. Nevertheless, I had this guy sign a one-year lease.

During that year, this guy's true colors would come out. When I went to collect the rent money the first month he decided to arbitrarily deduct money for a new door lock because he didn't want me coming into his apartment uninvited and so that is why I changed the locks, he told me. He never called me to inform me about changing the locks. He never gave a receipt to prove that he had actually spent the money on what he said he did. He had decided to paint some walls in the apartment without consulting with me, and charged me for the expenses. C was not helpful at all during this time that this guy was taking advantage of me and he never once spoke to him after I rented the apartment to him.

On one occasion I decided to go and see how he was keeping the apartment so I knocked on the door and he took a long time to answer the door but I waited and rang the doorbell again and again and he eventually came down to open the door. I asked him if I could come in and he allowed me. As I was walking up the stairs I immediately smelled marijuana and I assumed that is why he took a long time to open the door. I was so upset but did not let him see it. I did proceed to inform him that the neighborhood was a drug free neighborhood and that if I had known this about him I would not have rented the apartment to him. The apartment was a mess and dirty. I didn't like his attitude toward me, he was very disrespectful in the way he spoke to me. I told him that when the year's lease was up I would appreciate if he would move out. He turned to me and said in intimating manner, I was told by your ex-brother-in-law that I could stay and I'm not going to move out at your request. I knew at that point that I had a fight on my hands with my ex-brother-in-law.

I went to see my lawyer who warned me against going to court on a case like this so I decided that it was not worth it. I decided to sell my share of that property and left it alone. I was not about to lose my peace and joy over that property. I ended up selling and having to split the money with my son, who happened to be stationed at the Marine base in Camp Pendleton San Diego California at that time and with his half-brother, my late husband's first born.

Deep down I was so angry and sad that I had lost the property that had belonged to me and H for those 20 years. I failed to hold onto something that had meant so much to me and my children and grandchildren. I was definitely not happy with myself nor with C.

Several years later, I heard the rumor that there had been a fire in the basement (that tenant kept work equipment down there) and that he no longer lived there.

THE ADJACENT APARTMENT

I had received $25,000 for myself and I was in the position to find another apartment, get my marriage annulled and move on with my life but I don't know what actually happened to me or what I was doing at the time that I had received that money. I had to have been thinking about the business to have put off something as important as preserving my sanity. I was in the process of getting the hair salon ready and I know that it needed more work and money to purchase more materials. I believe that the business had taken priority over everything else.

However, I was fixing the back apartment adjacent to the shop so I thought that I would move in there when the job was done. That apartment that had been rented by a friend of H's brother. That friend had been involved in drugs "crack cocaine" and he demolished the apartment. He broke down walls and tore out electric fixtures, ripped out an entire toilet, it was a real mess in there. I don't know what happened to him. I know that my ex-brother in-law told me, I could have the business and the back apartment as part of H's share of the property. My thoughts were that if I fix the apartment then I would move into it and have the shop up and running and that way I would be all set.

CHAPTER 24

STRANGE OCCURRENCES

Finally, be strong in the Lord and in the strength of his might. Put on the whole armor of God, that you may be able to stand against the schemes of the devil. For we do not wrestle against flesh and blood, but against the rulers, against the authorities, against the cosmic powers over this present darkness, against the spiritual forces of evil in the heavenly places.

Ephesians 6:10-12, NLT

SATANIC INFLUENCES

I was only in our first apartment for one year and it wasn't because I did not want to live there any longer but because of the strange happenings that I began to observe in and around the apartment. It all started when the neighbors began to freak me out with their odd behavior. I thought it was a safe place which it appeared to be at first, but then something strange occurred after we came back from a vacation we took in May.

I started to look forward to taking vacations anytime to be happy and keep sane. So when C decided to take his vacation he invited me to come along. I thought it was a good idea, since my classes were over for that semester. We went to Florida to visit my brothers and sisters, who were not able to attend our wedding. We were gone for one week.

When we got back, I went to put my suitcase in my storage cage in the basement when I noticed that someone had made a mess of the storage next to mine and things that had been inside of it were outside by the other storage area. I noticed that the lock from my storage was gone. I checked to see if anything was missing but I couldn't remember half of the stuff I had down there. Anyway, I thought there was nothing personal or valuable they could have taken from there so I ignored the whole incident after reporting it to the office manager and the maintenance worker.

The maintenance guy didn't strike me as weird at first but he would be one of them. Strange things began to occur about two months after we had been back from vacation. We lived on the first floor and to the right of my apartment there lived an elderly Caucasian lady. She was about 5'4", very thin and ghostly pale looking. She walked so quietly that I was surprised and startled to see her behind me in the hallway one day. Her appearance scared me and I got goose bumps all over and the chills ran up and down my back, it's like she appeared out of nowhere.

Across from us lived a Caucasian couple, the female was a tall pretty-looking pale-skin woman with black shoulder length hair in her mid-thirties and her attractive male companion was short with black hair almost same age. Both would stare at me with these piercing eyes, sometimes grinning but most times a very serious stare. They were strange in my estimation.

Further down, two doors toward the other side of the long corridor lived a single Caucasian male. I assumed he was in his mid-fifties, with ashy-white skin. He stared at me until I would greet him and he responded with a nod and then went into his apartment. Directly above me, was a Caucasian stately-looking male and female couple in their late sixties. I assumed that they were retired.

The strangeness of these tenants reminded of the characters from the 1970's movie "Rosemary's Baby," that took place in a NYC apartment building and involved witchcraft and Satanism. They were a peculiar bunch with their bizarre stares, suspicious eyes and peculiar mannerisms. These tenants all gave me an eerie feeling whenever I was greeted by them in the hallway or by the stairs. They'd look at me intensely and I'd be filled with this immense fear that made my skin crawl. I couldn't make it into my apartment any faster to get away from them. I can't help but think about it now that maybe they saw something in me that I did not know that I possess. Maybe they actually saw the demons that I didn't know were there around me. Hey, anything is possible. I was not prepared for what Satan had in stored for me. But for the grace of God...

EVIL PRESENCE

Behold, I have given you authority to tread on serpents and scorpions, and over all the power of the enemy, and nothing shall hurt you.

Luke 10:19 (NLT)

One weekend my 9-year old step-daughter came to visit and she decided to stay over that night. The next morning, she told us that in the middle of the night, she opened her eyes to get up and use the toilet when she saw a man pass by her bedroom door toward our bedroom, which is towards the bathroom. She got scared, closed her eyes and kept on sleeping. I did not want to spook her so I did not mention that when I returned from Florida, I had suspected that someone had been in the apartment while we were away on vacation.

Whoever entered my apartment left an evil presence, that was very strong and creepy. I thought that I was imaging things but I call it having a discerning spirit. Whoever entered our apartment had been given permission from the maintenance worker who had keys to every apartment in the building. It happened right after our return from Florida that I started to sense that presence which caused me to lose sleep. Then, when she told us that story about the man I knew that someone had entered our apartment and whoever it was lived in the apartment building and had keys to get in and out of our apartment whenever they felt like it. Sometimes I would catch the upstairs couple hiding behind the curtains watching us as we'd leave to go to church on Wednesday evenings and on Sundays and on other occasions. I would call out to them and say hello to let them know that I knew they were watching us, I was polite.

Other strange occurrences happened like when I'd be in the bathroom getting ready to take a shower I'd feel a cold, freezer-like, breeze below the knees to the ankles as I would stand by the bathroom sink. I could never figure out where it was coming from. This happened in the winter even when we would have the heater on. There was no air-conditioner located in that area that would let out that kind of breeze.

One evening, we had to meet some friends for dinner and we were running late so we both decided to jump in the shower together when we both felt the cold breeze again. He told me that he had felt it on other occasions but never gave it any thought. We both decided to look together and find out where that cold wind or breeze was coming from so he took down a couple of the ceiling tiles and looked for cracks, holes, drafts but there were no visible vents or open spaces. Then he looked under the bathroom basin cabinet and nothing.

We both went down to the basement together, we were both scared. I could tell by his face that he was spooked. There were no holes or vents leading into our apartment and no openings to the outside. It struck me as weird that even while it was warm outside and hot in the apartment that I could still feel the coldness in that particular area. It would make my skin crawl and I feared that something evil was in my apartment. There was this frightening feeling that would come over me, like someone was watching me all the time, something diabolical. Every time I entered the building, I was filled with this strange fear that I couldn't understand, and I dreaded going into my apartment. I was alright while I was at work or elsewhere until it was time to go home.

Several months later, I decided that I would snoop around and get to the bottom of this. I'd try to catch the upstairs neighbors when they were coming into the building or when they were leaving to stop and talk to them but it was hard. There was one time that I thought I almost stopped them in the stairwell but they'd rushed upstairs so fast that I missed them. I still wanted to find out who were these people and what were they trying to do to me. So one day I decided to make friends with the 'ghostly' looking elderly lady and I knocked on her door with a plate with a few pieces of bread pudding and Puerto Rican style custard pudding. She took the plate but did not invite me into her apartment. She was not your typical old lady with the rosy cheeks and the happy smiles who would always invite you in her home for a hot chocolate or a lemonade. I would get a creepy feeling every time I saw her in the hallway. I thought I would try again some other time

It was November and I finally had the opportunity to go into her apartment. I knocked on the door and she invited me in and I made up some excuse to use her bathroom. I looked around and did not see anything out of the ordinary in her bathroom, the tiles were the same. I was actually looking to see if I was the only one with the tile ceilings. She kept a clean apartment (almost unlivable, it was too tidy) with the essential sofa and chair with the coffee table and the dollies on top. She had a table with a lamp that had fringes, (very antique looking). The shades were drawn down. Don't remember seeing curtains on the living room window. The walls were empty of picture frames and no decorations anywhere. I was so frightened that I can't remember what I spoke to her about I just wanted to leave her apartment. The whole experience was eerie.

I finally decided to get a burglar alarm for my apartment. I went to Home Depot and bought a cheaply one that I had to glue on the door myself since it was not my property I couldn't install a professional alarm system. The purpose was to stop unwanted strangers from coming into my apartment. It made this loud and annoying noise. If someone came in uninvited and didn't know the code to shut it off, it would stay on forever. I intentionally tested it one evening and most of the tenants came out of their apartments to see what the noise was about and I told them, "I am just testing my burglar alarm." They all looked annoyed, and I just wanted to let them know that they better not come into my apartment without permission. So I set up the alarm and felt reassured that no one would come into the apartment unless invited.

I'M HOOKED LIKE A FISH!

Over the Thanksgiving holidays, we went to Puerto Rico so that I could meet his mother, sister, and nephew and niece. When I met my new in-laws I immediately fell in love with them. His mother a woman with fair complexion who kept her black-dyed hair back in a bun and she dressed very mod-est. She is of the Pentecostal faith. His sister has a dark com-plexion, black straight long hair and looks like a descendent of the Taino Indians. The **Taíno** were an Arawak people who were the indigenous people of the Caribbean and Florida. C told me that his great grandmother was full breed Taino.

Puerto Rico is a beautiful island and it's not hard to fall in love with it. I started to dream about buying a house there for when I retire from work I can visit for a few months and grow my vegetables and herbs. I looked at land and property for sale but I didn't have the money to purchase land. I was taken aback with the beauty that this island has and I didn't want to come back home. I was very appreciative of him for taking me there and he promised to take me back the following year. I was ecstatic. I had been to Puerto Rico several times before but not the west coast. It's very beautiful. He took me on a tour of the North and West coast of the Island. I went swimming at Crashboat beach known, for its colorful boats and for surfing. I visited San Sebastian Market town where the green plantains are bigger than my arm in length. And lastly I went to Camuy River Cave Park. I enjoyed eating the typical Island cuisine, and the weather couldn't have been any better, some 80 degrees every day. And of course, the Latin rhythms of the Island music was entertaining. I also got some shopping done. I can't leave Puerto Rico without buying a few pairs of summer sandals from "LA GLORIA" shoe store.

He had hooked me like a fish when he took me to Puerto Rico and now I definitely could not just walk away from all of this because who will bring me back and where would I stay, if not with his family. I still don't know who is behind all of these distractions. I am being enticed and guided away from God's calling and purpose.

I had to go back to the reality of things. The cold weather awaited me as well as my school, and my job; and that awful eerie place where I was living.

It was our first Christmas in that apartment and our families came to visit. One evening as we are all enjoying each other's company, there was knock at the door. When I opened the door it was the old lady who came to bring me some cookies that she had made. I thanked her for the cookies and invited her to come in but she stayed at the door and I can't remember what she said but she left. I'm sorry to say that I could not eat those cookies for fear that they were cursed or something. I never saw her again after that visit, it's as if she had vanished after that night.

However, my suspicions about what was happening in that apartment building with my neighbors did not go unfounded. I was curious because she never said goodbye. After all she did bring me cookies and we did exchange greetings in the hallway. So I asked the maintenance guy who told me, "She moved out" and he left it at that and walked away from me. That was creepy.

GOD'S ANGELS

For the angel of the LORD is a guard; he surrounds and defends all who fear him. Psalm 34:7 (NLT)

I finally moved out in March of the following year but I had to return to the apartment afterwards to do some patch work on the walls where I had hung pictures. C had been too busy with his work and he couldn't take the time out so he left it up to me to go there all by myself. I thought how dare he allow me to do this alone, knowing how I couldn't wait to move from there and how I had been creeped out living there.

Anyway, I had no choice because I would not get my Security Deposit back if I didn't make the repairs. As I was walking into the building I ran into the partner of the woman who lived across from us and there he is chest to chest with me. He is standing there for some time and is blocking me form moving forward and he had this diabolic smile on his face. I was not afraid at that point and I looked at him with a defiant stare and he stepped aside so that I could pass but he kept his eyes on me until I disappeared into the apartment. I had prayed before going into that building and God gave me the boldness and the fear was gone.

I had just finished compounding the holes in the walls, I never heard him come in but there I am face to face with the maintenance guy, and he is all in my space, face to face, almost touching noses but I did not back down and was not afraid of him because I felt the presence of God with me. I stared him straight in his eyes and gave him the apartment keys and left. That was a strange and unexpected occurrence since I never mentioned to him or anyone that I was coming over to the apartment, but somehow I got the feeling that they both knew. He had a sneaky look on his face but I smiled at him and told him, "goodbye," and walked right out of the apartment and out of that building with the confidence that God's angels had protected me from a satanic attack. I believe to this day that there was something satanic about that building and those tenants and the maintenance guy. I felt the strong presence of evil there.

I must say that the whole time I lived in that apartment I lived in fear and I had difficulty sleeping. I did not have a good night's sleep because all night long I would spend it rebuking evil spirits; their presence was so strong I thought that I would lose my mind. I'd see dark shadows lurking in the corner of my bedroom and hear loud banging noises at night. C would hear it but it didn't seem to bother him at all, he just kept right on sleeping. Whenever he talked about going on vacation I jumped and went, it was the only way that I could've gotten a good night sleep; being away from that apartment. I know that it was God who kept me that entire year from losing my mind. Looking back at that situation I did not have the spiritual strength I needed because I had taken my eyes off of God, who is my strength. But God in His infinite mercy kept me.

CHAPTER 25

THE CRITIC

"Let the day of my birth be erased, and the night I was conceived. (Job 3:3, NLT)

REGRETS!

I needed money for my tuition and the salon project to get it up and running. I started using up all the credit cards I owned. I had a 401K savings account that I didn't want to touch because it was my emergency money and I also had a savings account for my necessary expenses that I didn't want to spend. I was living on my bi-weekly paycheck, still paying for my school tuition and paying the expenses incurred by the hair salon to keep it up to city codes. The vacations that we took would be on credit cards and that had to be paid eventually. When it came to paying the rent and the two security deposits on our next apartment I had to go into my savings account and all because I wanted to live in a decent neighborhood like I had gotten accustomed to. The rents were higher and that was the price I had to pay. I started to blame myself for marrying someone outside of the will of God. I began to regret the decisions I had made. I would entertain the thoughts of when I had the property and how I would be in my own home living rent free since the mortgage had been paid off the same year that I got married and all I would be paying for would be the taxes and house insurance. I begin to criticize myself for my foolishness and it had brought me to where I was paying rent and using up my savings. This was our second year of marriage and we're moving into our first condominium in Shelton. There is a swimming pool in the complex which I looked forward to utilizing. It was a beautiful apartment, very modern, cozy and just right for the both of us.

WHERE'S THE LOVE?

I bought new living room furniture because I didn't like his old set and my son was moving into his new apartment, so I told him he could have C's furniture. I had asked C to buy the furniture for me, but I ended up paying the entire bill with my income tax. It made me feel better to treat myself to a new set of furniture and live in a beautiful apartment.

However, that still did not make up for the void that I felt in my heart of being truly loved by someone. I knew that he was not that someone, he didn't know how. Several months into our relationship, by his own admission, he told me that he didn't know how to be a husband, it was never taught to me, he said. I didn't know what to say but I thought, well I'll have to teach him. Yeah right!

I was still looking for a way out of my marriage but there was nowhere to go except to the apartment behind the shop but my son who was discharged from the Marines had moved into that apartment with his family and I could not very well tell the tenants on the other two floors to move out, so I had to wait it out a little longer.

In the meanwhile, I enjoyed my new apartment with its new furniture, the swimming pool that I used frequently. I'd invite my friends and family over for dinner and we'd listen to music, and that made it all the more bearable, living the lie. Even though on several occasions I'd try to tell him that our marriage wasn't ordained by God he wouldn't listen to me. While we lived in that apartment we took two vacations together. One was a cruise to the Caribbean and the other was a trip to Mexico to celebrate our one-year wedding anniversary. I took a vacation by myself to Florida to visit my relatives from my paternal side of the family; I spent a week there. I was still in school and had one more year until graduation and sometimes I just needed to get away from it all to relax my mind, and get some sleep. I had continued to spend my nights rebuking evil spirits that kept me up at night. I became more and more fearful and it all started to affect my mind to where I really thought that I would lose it. I felt that whatever, whoever it was wanted me to lose my mind. I started to hate my existence. But I was too afraid to admit that I had invited the enemy into my life and in my home so I suppressed the thought. I felt like my life was being wasted by being in that marriage and that I was a miserable excuse for a human. I had begun to hate being me.

I WANT OUT!

We went to Mexico to celebrate our first wedding anniversary and he encouraged me to buy a Timeshare and promised me that he would help me pay for it. Like a fool, I bought it and it cost me a pretty penny until I told him to take it and that I wasn't I going to pay for it any longer. I spent about four years paying for something that we never used. and I had to take out two hundred fifty dollars from my check once a month when I could have been saving that money. What a foolish person I had become and that was why I wanted out of this marriage because I knew deep down in my soul that I had done the wrong thing. God had tried to warn me and I refused to listen.

Eventually, there were going to be many truths that I would discover about C and myself. I still believed in the Ten Commandments, "Thou shalt not lie." I continued to attend my church before switching to his church on his whim. The last time I went to my church, I happened to have ran into my admirer/church brother and his girlfriend and we sat next them and he introduced his girlfriend to us.

On C's birthday, his youngest daughter gave him a surprise birthday gift that had been wrapped in a shirt box and I'm watching him open it thinking that it was a shirt of sort. It had been tied with multicolored ribbons and filled with an excess of multicolored tissue paper inside and when he finally looked inside and pulled out the gift he began to weep. It was an 8x10 photo of his dead younger brother. He could not look at it and asked me to put it away where he will never see again. That had been the first time I had the opportunity to see a photo of his younger brother and when I saw the face on the frame, I was shocked to see that he was the same young male I had seen in my dream that night at C's apartment two years earlier. I began to imagine all sorts of weird things about him and how sensitive and teary-eyed he would get when remembering his brother's death. He had been the only witness to the drowning incident.

Stay alert! Watch out for your great enemy, the devil. He prowls around like a roaring lion, looking for someone to devour. 1 Peter 5:8 (NLT)

I CAN'T SLEEP...

I found it very difficult to sleep next to C because of the heat his body gave out. In addition to all the other strange things I had to deal with at night, that was just as bad because I felt as thou I were suffocating. The only time that I didn't mind being next to him was during the cold months because the nights were cold, but it would be only for a little while. I started to think if he had escaped a burning inferno and I wanted to know if this was a figment of my imagination or if emission of body heat ran in his family.

I had become very good friends with C cousin's wife, He was the best man at our wedding, and I felt comfortable asking her one day about him and his sleeping habits. I was trying to investigate certain characteristics and behavior of his relatives that somehow would explain something about him, so that I would stop looking at him like an alien from outer space or a demon. C had told me some stories about several traffic accidents he had the past twenty years (before we met) that were life threatening and he survived them by some miracle. The first was a motorcycle accident at age eighteen, hitting a nine-year old boy killing him instantly. I tried very hard to avoid hitting the little boy, he told me. The second was driving an oil tanker and it rolled over. The EMT told him the driver should have been killed. The third was unexplainable. He told me that he died for several minutes. I almost surely believed that C had been saved by God for a greater purpose but I saw it differently at the time because I felt spooked by it all.

I don't know if this had any relevance to why I couldn't sleep next to him or why he was the person he was. So in our second year of marriage I had made up in my mind that with the help of the Holy Spirit and His angels, I'd sleep with the peace of God and I'd have nothing to fear. But stranger things continued to occur, even with believing in God and praying day and night.

CHAPTER 26

LOST MY WAY

⁶ My people have been lost sheep… They have lost their way and can't remember how to get back to the sheepfold. ⁷ All who found them devoured them. (Jeremiah 50:6-7, NLT)

CHANGED CHURCH

I had been happy with the condo, and I wouldn't have minded renting for another year. My research paper was coming along great. My friends and family visited often and we'd hangout by the pool or have dinner and listen to music. I was still looking forward to opening up the "Resurrection Hair Salon." I had recently become the proud owner of a three family house. I had purchased the property on Fairfield Avenue in Bridgeport where the salon stood. I didn't have any problems with the tenants because they paid their rent on time which paid the mortgage.

I had started to attend the Spanish church with C because he insisted that a wife should attend church with her husband. His church was located on the east side of Bridgeport, a historical site. It was a quaint old church with a center bell steeple, concrete steps that lead to the entrance. The sanctuary was on the upper level and the fellowship hall on the bottom. After about a year of attending his church, I got acquainted with most of the members and fell in love with most of them. I was called to usher in the church and do the hospitality ministry on some Sundays. I volunteered in the nursery and sometimes I helped with the cooking and serving.

During those years at this church, I had completely forgotten about my purpose and the reason God had lead me to my own church several years earlier. As I look back to that time I really can't remember how I lost sight of that. It's as if my memory had been erased in some way. But there I was attending another church instead of my own church.

NOT HAPPY

I was still unhappy in my marriage and I didn't like being married. I kept on contemplating the idea of leaving someday. I wanted to have my own home. I wanted to be loved as a woman should be loved, admired and wanted not just for sex. I knew that I was a good, faithful and a hard working woman that any man would have been proud to be married to. God had tried to tell me not to get involved with him and I did not listen to God. I refused to listen. I closed my ears to God's warnings and did not take heed to his words. I should have waited because I am sure God had someone especially for me.

Unfortunately, the landlord from the condo did not renew our lease and we had to move out. I had really liked the place and was hoping that she would have given us another year. She had decided she wanted to move back to her condo and stop paying rent elsewhere, which was understandable. I had to start looking for another apartment and I wanted to stay in that area of Shelton. I enjoyed the that it gave me some stability.

I ventured down a little further into Shelton to where I would still have access to that part of town. I was blessed to find a duplex only ten minutes away in a good, decent neighborhood. The house came with a good size yard to have picnics and have a small four by six rubber pool for the grandkids in the summer. It had a basement with a washer and dryer hook up and a big garage for storage. The house was located in almost a cul-de-sac, not too much traffic except for the residents driving to their homes. There were three bedrooms upstairs with a full bath, and the living room was big enough to fit my new sofa, chairs and tables. I especially liked the huge kitchen with sliding French doors that led to a good size patio. The rent was reasonable when split in half. I was excited to move in.

Since the kitchen was big enough, I wanted to buy a kitchen table that seated six with the matching hutch. I invited him to go with me to my favorite furniture store so that he could buy it for me, thinking that he would actually pay for it. But I was wrong again and I ended up having to pay for it myself, using my income tax money. Every piece of furniture we've had including the bedroom set in the apartment, I had to pay for.

He had a giving and kind heart and would buy me things that I wanted and sometimes surprise me with things but when it came to the essentials, I had to pay for them myself. He paid for his television set and he was excessively generous when it came to his children. C was and is an exceptional father and not to mention an exceptional friend.

I ALWAYS LOST...

The many vacations that we took in a year was because he wanted to get away from the stress of work even when we couldn't afford them but he'd manage to pay off all his credit cards, he had that knack. I would go with him because since that was the only thing that kept me sane in this marriage.

I will never forget how costly the vacation I took to Mexico was. I could never recover from losses like he did. I was always losing out. I felt like I was slowly being sucked clean of all I had saved and stored for a rainy day. I also felt like my life was wasting away. My life had become so pathetic. My thoughts kept badgering me about what a loser I had become and that I was being used and abused. I wanted out of this marriage so bad because I knew deep down in my soul that I had done wrong in the sight of God. God had already told me the why. But I was too afraid to admit that I had invited the evil one into my life and into my home. Come to think about it, how did I ever come up with a name like resurrection for the salon? Was God trying to tell me something because He only knows that I needed to be resurrected because I had been dead in my sin.

"My child, don't lose sight of common sense and discernment. Hang on to them." Proverbs 3:21 (NLT)

CHAPTER 27

DISOBEDIENCE

"The LORD was angry with Israel and made them wander in the wilderness for forty years until the entire generation that sinned in the Lord's sight had died." Numbers 32:13 (NLT)

UNGODLY THINKING

I remember a time when I had been stable in my own home for twenty-one years. But in this marriage, I was moving into my third apartment in three years, and I felt like a nomad wandering in the desert, but only in my case it was moving from apartment to apartment. I thought about the people of Israel when they were made to wonder the desert for forty years because of their disobedience.

My disobedience and rebellious attitude had caused me to roam the desert until the day that I acknowledged what I had done. I was married to C but I was subjected to Satan the hour that I told God "I don't care." I felt like I was alone, lost, without a map to guide me.

I was still attending church and seeking God morning and night. I paid my tithes and gave my offering, and got involved in church activities. I had told myself to live with it until I found a way out. I'd invite the church members over to the house for picnics and holiday parties and that made me happy but it still was not right what I was doing. I would pray to God to help get me out of this marriage. How foolish of me to think that I'd even consider asking God for such a thing as divorce. Anyway, my inner voice would tell me that Christians just didn't get divorce for no apparent reason unless there had been adultery and I was not about to commit outright adultery and neither would he. Sometimes I'd wished that he would have committed adultery so that I could have had a reason to divorce him. That was not Christ-like thinking. I'd listen to the Christian radio station and hear from Pastors talk about the alarming divorce rates among Christians and that would deter me from divorcing him.

THERAPY SESSIONS

I had decided to seek professional counseling to help me figure out what to do about my marriage. When we moved to the townhouse in our third year of marriage, I needed to discuss our sex life, our over spending, the lack of communication between us; and the decisions he made about important issues without consulting me first; his angry outbursts, and the stronghold that his children and their mothers had on him which interfered with the finances in the house. I had already been to see the therapist twice before to discuss these concerns and the therapist had suggested that I invite him to the third session and he agreed to attend, reluctantly of course, but we both showed up for the session.

When we arrived at the office, the therapist suggested that I see her first, I was not sure why, and I'm not sure what we talked about before she asked him in to the office. Then we talked about a variety of things, especially the things I had mentioned. He admitted that he had done and said most of what I had told the therapist about. He told the therapist that he would try to improve in those areas. The session was over.

As we were leaving the office, he was extremely quiet and on the way back to the house, he was very angry and told me that both, the therapist and I, had forced him to come to this session and that he felt attacked by us women. That was not true of course, but that was his opinion. He would not come back to anymore therapy sessions unless it was someone he could relate to, he thought that a male therapist would side with him more than the female therapist. Because in his mind he thought and he expressed it verbally that "women stick together." I could not get him to come back to another therapy session with this therapist or any other therapist, at least this year but I did try again the following year.

The following year I encouraged him to go with me to Pastoral counseling for the sake of saving my sanity first and foremost and to give our marriage a chance if I was to stay in it. I wanted to make sure that before I divorced him, I had exhausted every means to somehow save the marriage and therefore not feel guilty about the divorce actions that I would later take against him.

We both attended two counseling sessions and I saw that it was going nowhere, or benefitting neither one of us. He would sit in the session and keep his mouth shut the whole time while I did all of the talking and I thought that I was being viewed as "the bad guy." He would look like the injured party, so I gave up trying and told the couple that he would never get it and that it had been a waste of time for us all. I had done my best and did most if not all of the sacrificing in the marriage to salvage it but to no avail; so I stopped trying.

SOMETHING UGLY

After all my efforts to make things right in this marriage. I had awakened something ugly in him from the person that I had met years earlier. In that year of our marriage, his behavior was scary to say the least. There was an ugly side to him that I had never seen before. Sometimes I'd imagine that he wished me dead so that he would collect on the huge Life Insurance policy he bought the very first year that we got married.

I started to notice that my nights in our new home got worse and I continued to experience the heavy presence of evil in the house especially in my bedroom; and I'd spend most of the night rebuking those demons. Once again, something strange began to happen to me that had not happened before and it appeared to have escalated to the point that I felt my physical health was now in danger. For example, while I'd be sleeping at night I would feel as if someone or something was grabbing my heart and squeezing it until I'd wake up grasping for air. I'd noticed that if I slept facing him it would happen more frequently than if I faced away from him and I would not get that sensation of suffocating as much. We shared a king size bed and I would always sleep as far away from him as possible, even from the beginning of our marriage. I just didn't want to be his wife any longer because there was no romance between us.

At first, I didn't think much about what was happening to me in my own bedroom. I thought that it was because I was sleeping on the second floor and that height somehow had something to do with the tightness in my chest. However, it didn't make sense because I had also been sleeping in a second floor apartment when we lived in the condominium and I didn't feel like that back then. So, I continued to pray at night and rebuke evil spirits during my sleep. This situation was robbing me of rest which caused me to sleep a little longer in the morning, making me late for work almost every day. I was running out of excuses and my work evaluations were affected.

Those four years living in that third location were the most frustrating, infuriating and painful years of my marriage. It was when he exposed his ugly side that I never would have imagined he had. It was not helping our marriage. He became so verbally offensive toward me that not even I could believe the things that were coming out of his month. For example, he would say things like, I regret having met you, you are evil, and he would scream at me at the top of his lungs. Sometimes I thought he would hit me with his fist, and I became afraid of him.

IGNORE THE PROBLEM

Meanwhile, I thought that I would keep the peace and be the humble wife and try not to let anyone know that this was happening at home. I didn't want to spoil it since at that time we had such a great group of brothers and sisters from the church and I feared, that if I left him, I would also lose my church family and valued their company very much. Most of them were married couples and I enjoyed having them come over to the house for dinners, picnics and Christmas parties. I didn't want to ruin that. So, I decided to live with his behavior. I had made my bed, I had to sleep in it. I'd tell myself that my situation was temporary and that one day, I would be moving out. But in the meantime, I decided to ignore his behavior because the vacations he paid for made up for it and having the company of my church family was important to me. He believed there was no problem so there was no reason for him to change and if there was a problem, it problem was with me.

CHAPTER 28

THE RESURRECTION
HAIR SALON

"My thoughts are nothing like your thoughts, says the Lord. And my ways are far beyond anything you could imagine. For just as the heavens are higher than the earth, so my ways are higher than your ways and my thoughts are higher than your thoughts." Isaiah 55:8-9 (NLT)

MY BUSINESS

The business and the property became my main priority. I thought that in order to maintain my sanity, I'd put all my energy and concentration on my multi-family property and get into landlord mode. I began painting the hallways, installing carpet in the third floor apartment, buying the tenants cans of paint to use in their apartments. I also got involved in the hair salon project which kept me focused on something that satisfied me and was all mine. I'd stop by during the weekdays after work and some weekends to see the progress. The salon was coming along very well as all the work that it needed was completed, finally after three years. The reason that it took that long to complete was due to the bad New England winter that we had during those last two years. The winter would last from November to April, almost every year after the work had begun at the shop in 2004. There was no heating system installed in the shop and the freezing weather would make it unbearable for the man to work. So they would work from May into October during those years. The shop would be up and running no later than September of 2007. The investment I made toward the shop was worth it I thought. I was so impressed with the work the guys had done into putting down the wood floor. I had bought four work stations that were setup in the center of the salon with salon chairs and the sinks and hair dryers that were ready to be used. The sinks were against the left wall where I wanted them and the hair dryers were in their place against the wall, straight ahead as you entered the business. I had the three-foot wall put up for the purpose of sheltering women while they were drying their hair. I had the workers put benches along the front windows for customers to sit down while they waited their turn. Still I needed to get the cushions for the benches, the hair products and styling supplies. I had an old sign that I was going to reuse for the new name "The Resurrection Hair Salon," and all I needed was the money to contract the graphic designer. The shops city codes were up to regulation. I was using up most of the credit on my Home Depot card. It reached about ten thousand dollars from a sixteen thousand credit line.

MY PLANNING

I had told myself that the property and the business would pay itself off, and that I would pay off my personal credit card that I had taken cash advances on to pay the workers with my income tax check. I was not worried about getting the personnel because I had already spoken to two young ladies from church that had completed their cosmetology classes and were licensed. They had already been working for a salon and both were eager to work for me.

The Resurrection Hair Salon was to be a place where people came to get their hair done and receive spiritual wisdom at the same time. It was my intention of making it a place of refuge for the lost and for evangelism. For example, I'd have Christian music playing all the time on the DVD player, and have wall plaques with scriptures hanging everywhere in the shop; and have religious tracks for customers to take with them.

I had met this artist in H's church, when I was attending it, and I befriended him. He had agreed to paint a mural on the wall outside the shop, on the right. It was to be painted in baby blue like the sky with one or two medium sized white clouds and a ray of bright golden light coming from heaven; with a few doves flying around and a scripture from the Bible like Psalm 23 or The Lord's Prayers. I wanted the customers and passer-by to read it as they went by the shop. I was very excited about owning a shop and using it for God's glory. I was already sharing the Gospel with one of my tenants. I had it all worked out, so I thought. It made me happy to be doing Kingdom work.

MY ASSUMPTION

I had been working under the assumption that all of what I was doing was for God's glory and to save the lost souls on that side of town.

Somewhere in the back of my mind I knew that this was not what God had called me in the Northeast for but I figured that since I would be evangelizing it would be alright with God. We can never assume what God thinks and what He will accept. We should never assume that God will meet us halfway. We would be taking the God of the universe for granted and that is unacceptable.

CHAPTER 23

TWO THOUSAND SEVEN

They did not keep God's covenant and refused to live by his instructions.

Psalm 78:10 (NLT)

I WILL NEVER FORGET

It was December 7 of 2007 a date I will never forget. I was awakened by a faint voice calling my name and I heard it repeated several times, "Mona, Mona, Mona." But feeling the way I did I ignored it the first few times. It was C trying to wake me up at 4 in the morning to tell me that my Fairfield Avenue property was on fire. My first response to him was "I am so sick, let me sleep," obviously I had not grasped what he was saying to me.

I was in bed with the flu, chills, fever, body aches, pounding headache and pain all over. I could hardly move my body so I really didn't want to hear that kind of news at that time. Then he said, "the tenants don't have anywhere to go and the police officer is asking for you." I then thought about my son and his family who were living in the first floor apartment in the back. I thought I better get up and take care of my responsibility as a landlord.

I got up and bundled myself up with sweaters, long johns, scarves, gloves; a hat plus a hoodie and boots and headed out to Bridgeport with C driving his truck. When I got out into the street it was freezing, it had to be in the single digits that night.

When we arrived both my property and the house next door were on fire. The flames were shooting out into the sky of my third floor apartment. The fire department was there battling the fire trying hard to stop it but the cold weather and wind factor was not helping. Water was freezing up within the fire hose. They tried very hard to contain the fire to the two properties, trying to prevent the others houses from burning.

The right section of my house, which was the closest to the other burning house, burned significantly. The third floor of my house burned completely down on the entire right side, half of the apartment on the second floor burned down and the first floor got excessive water damage as did the business. The house to the right burned down completely. That night, I was out in that freezing weather until seven thirty in the morning making sure that the tenants had somewhere to stay. The Red Cross gave the tenants and everyone else around hot cocoa and blankets to keep them warm. I took the hot cocoa and blanket since I was sick. I needed it. They also assisted the tenants with finding shelter in a nearby hotel. My son and his family were not in their apartment that night, thank God.

I assisted the fire department the best I could. They needed my permission to go into my property and break down fences and retaining walls to get to the house next door from the back yard. That house was about fifty feet from my property. I was told that the fire had started in the house next door, and that there was a freak accident in the basement. Someone in the house had constructed a makeshift fireplace to keep warm and it blew up setting it on fire and the flames from that house set the whole side of my house on fire. Everything got ruined in the fire. I was not going to invest again buying furniture for the hair salon. Thank God all the tenants survived the fire and were relocated.

MAJOR TRAGEDY

The story of how the house blew up was told by the surviving family members. It was in the Connecticut Post that following day. There were about twenty people living in the basement of that property, illegally, and there were no heaters down there and they decided to make a fire place to stay warm using gasoline.

When the house blew up it was immediately engulfed in flames. How the people that were in the basement got out is still a mystery. The husband ran out of the house with his two teenage boys and when he noticed that his wife and 18-month old child were not outside. He ran back inside to get them and when they were about to run out of the house the entire second floor fell on them. The firefighters found him on top of her and her on top of the baby near the front doorway, apparently he had been trying to shield them from the falling ceiling. It was a major tragedy for the survivors of that family and somewhat of a tragedy for me in that my dream had gone up in smoke. The shop that had become my priority had been burned.

I WANT A DIVORCE

That same year, I told C that our marriage had been a mistake from the very beginning and that I wanted a divorce. He kept denying that our marriage was a mistake and was not willing to give me the divorce. He had made up his mind that our marriage was arranged by God. He claimed that I was put in his life to save him from his destructive life style.

Back when I first started dating him, I did not know that he smoked cigarettes and when I found out I told him that it was over between us and I gave him back the engagement ring and ran out of the apartment. I should have kept on running. But he chased me and promised that he would quit and he did. He believed that I had been an angel in disguise to help save his life. But now he would scream at the top of his lungs and tell me, I was a demon sent from hell to destroy his peace. In turn, I believed that he was the demon sent from hell to destroy me but I never said the words.

There were many times that we'd scream at each other some really hurtful things. I argued with him about spending his share of the rent and how I had to pay the entire rent that month. I would tell him time and time to stop spending his money on things without talking to me first. He had changed considerably and I did not like the person he had become. I could not have a conversation with him that did not turn into an argument. I tried to build him up but he thought that I was treating him like an idiot. Sometimes I wanted to punch him in his face and break his teeth, not godly thinking or behavior. I was made to feel like the bully, and I was disliking him more and more each day.

CHAPTER 30

I LOST IT ALL...

"Trust in your money and down you go!
But the godly flourish like leaves in spring."

Proverbs 11:28 (NLT)

INSURANCE MONEY...REBUILT

It snowed the whole month of December way into February of 2008 and there was nothing that could be done about the property until the weather got warmer. I had to wait until the insurance adjuster examined the damages to collect the insurance money to start work on the property. There was extensive damage to the house and everything in the shop was ruined by the water and a lot of fallen debris. What the fire didn't destroy was stolen by the neighborhood thieves.

I finally received a check from the insurance company after eight months of going back and forth with them. By now, I'm eight months behind on my mortgage payments. I asked the lawyer who helped with the closing on the property and he suggested that I don't spend the money on anything else. That was helpful but not what I was looking for to move forward and fix the house.

I paid the bank first and with the remaining balance, I reserved it to pay the new contractors to start rebuilding my house. I didn't want to go to C for advice, although he knew many contractors. I did not trust the people he'd referred to me because of my earlier experience when he referred his good friend and I ended up losing my home in Stratford. Not knowing who else to seek for help, I asked him because I had no choice at that point. He found a couple of contractors that he claimed he trusted because one of them had done work for him in the past. I was afraid of contractors who would take the money and not finish the job but I was assured that these guys wouldn't do that.

These contractors were charging me a small fraction of what others contractors were asking for so I agreed to sign a contract with them. He wanted contractors that would only rebuild the inside of the property and put the roof back on the house. He and his workers would fix the outside, such as the roof, windows, aluminum siding and gutters. He fought me not to hire outside contractors to do what his business could do and I gave in, since he was my husband.

The work on the property began 13 months after the fire. In January of 2009 I asked C if he could oversee the work being done to the property because I was working over half an hour away in Waterbury.

I received my Master's degree in May of 2007 and was promoted to Clinical Social Worker and was transferred to the Northwest CT Mental Health Network in that city. I depended on him to do this for me since he was in the vicinity and his work allowed him that flexibility and I was giving these two guys huge amounts of money to buy material and for their labor. I should have taken heed of what these guys were all about when one of contractors had told me that he was going to buy property in Virginia. I found out that he had left the work undone at the property to go on vacation to Virginia as soon as I gave him a check for $23,000 and when he came back he asked me for another $23,000 to complete his work on the house. The other contractor was always asking for more money as well.

I heard from the heating and refrigeration guy that the second contractor was spending most of my money across the street at the "strip joint." I would visit the property and for the most part it looked as if nothing had been done to it. To make a long story short, the contractors never finished the work on the property, and they took off with most of my money. All I had left was a shell of a house that was gutted inside and unlivable. I did not have any more money from the insurance money to repair the house and I refused to use the money from my 401K.

401K MONEY... SALVAGE IT

I did not want to fail a second time and lose this property as well so I tried to salvage it for the sake of my children. I decided to go to my 401K and I made a withdrawal of ten thousand dollars. I had hired another contractor, who I had met at my church, and he did try to finish the work but I ran out of money so I had to stop the work and eventually the bank took the house. At first I blamed C for losing both of the properties that I had inherited from H. I was very disappointed with him, especially when he told me several years later that he really didn't know those two contractors at all. I wonder why he would tell me to give them the job. I felt that I could not depend on him anymore and had lost all confidence in him.

PERSONAL MONEY... NEW VENTURE

Think about the things of heaven, not the things of earth
Colossians 3:2 (NLT)

Months before I lost the house to the bank, I had received an extra ten thousand from the insurance company for personal damages and it was all mine to use it as I pleased. I had to intentions on spending it on the property.

My friend, who had been my hairdresser for nine years, was opening a funeral home and was looking for someone to buy her salon since she couldn't run both businesses at the same time. I told her that I had received this money and with her encouragement I bought the shop from her. She asked for thirty-five thousand with the ten thousand as the deposit. The shop had been there for sixteen years and it was well established with longtime customers and there were plenty of supplies so I did not have any worries. I was not the business woman I thought that I was but I gave it a try. I thought that since the shop on Fairfield Avenue burned down, I could use this one for my intended purpose of evangelizing and this was the right neighborhood to start. Most of the people in the area were from low-income families. The shop was located on Park Avenue in Bridgeport near Seaside Park. There was a low-income housing project across the street from the shop. The inside of the shop had two sides to it, the retail area and the salon side with work stations where the customers had their hair done. The shop sold many different things like hair products, wigs, blow-dryers, hats, gloves and scarves (these items only sold during the winter months), and it even sold real gold and costume jewelry. The shop had five employees and each had their own customers but also took walk-ins.

I knew nothing about the business but the salon manager was to help me and I trusted her since she had been there for thirteen years. I was still working at my regular job, 40 minutes away and did not know what was going on at the shop during operating hours. I couldn't get my family to help me with the shop because they had their own jobs, not even on weekends were they able to show up. I could only stop in on Friday evenings and all day Saturday. It was closed on Sundays. I struggled with the maintenance of the shop and the employees were not easy characters to work with. I came to realize that I could not afford to pay their salaries, for the loan, and the rent, and buy the hair supplies needed to keep the salon running. I was putting more money into the business from my pocket than what it was making.

MONEY DON'T BUY HAPPINESS...

I'd argue with C about his lack of interest in what interested me. Every time I'd ask him for help with the shop it turned into an argument and I'd have to pay an outsider to do the work. My family and my friends did not come to assist me when I needed them. I felt completely alone. What happened to my world of peace, love, and joy? I thought this shop would be my opportunity to move on with my life and get away from my dependence on C. I closed the shop exactly one year from the time I opened it. I thank God that the landlord allowed me to break the three-year lease provided that I leave him the keys to the shop and all the equipment.

It was obvious that when we depend on mankind to come through for you they will leave you wanting. But God... I learned something very valuable in that God is that friend that never quits, He is a friend indeed.

There are "friends" who destroy each other, but a real friend sticks closer than a brother. Proverbs 18:24 (NLT)

Every avenue that I went down would only lead back to my dependence on C. Whatever was holding me captive was beyond my control. I had no clue as to what 'it' was.

CHAPTER 31

LORD HELP ME KEEP MY SANITY

²⁸ Then Jesus said, "Come to me, all of you who are weary and carry heavy burdens, and I will give you rest. ²⁹ Take my yoke upon you. Let me teach you, because I am humble and gentle at heart, and you will find rest for your souls. ³⁰ For my yoke is easy to bear, and the burden I give you is light." Matthew 11:28-30 (NLT)

LORD, FREE ME

I had lost all I had inherited from H as well as the business that I had ventured into. I had mixed feelings about this loss in that I was relieved that I didn't have to go to court over the property rental lease but I was angry and saddened that I had lost the properties that were meant to be for my children and grandchildren. I had my suspicion that my sin had something to do with all the previous losses, and that my marriage to C had put a stop to the true calling in my life. God had other plans for me and I rejected them the night I rebelled against him. I chose to sin instead. That decision put me in a bad place, in a bad marriage, with evil spirits that relentlessly persecuted me. How was I going to turn this situation around? I knew that I had betrayed God and I tried hard to make up for it but I knew that I was living in sin because I didn't love the man I was married to. Yet I would go on vacation with him as if everything was alright only because I was satisfying my own desires, and that was very deceitful and wrong in God's eyes. I was being enticed and distracted from following my God, my Lord and Savior. Sure, I attended church and prayed and tithed but I was living a lie.

Something more sinful began to arise in me toward the middle of our fourth year of marriage. It had to do with lusting after other men. I was committing adultery with my mind. I was so unhappy that I wanted someone else's husband to make me happy. I sometimes had thoughts of being a widow again so that I would be free to marry again. These sinful thoughts were not normal for a Christian to be having and I knew that something was terribly wrong with my spiritual life.

The only time that I felt free was when I'd go on vacation alone. It was an excuse to run from all of the madness that enveloped me at times. I had to do this very frequently during my marriage to keep myself sane. I had imprisoned myself with my own two hands.

I remember going to church one Saturday morning for intercessory prayer (I found peace there.) During one of the many issues and concerns raised in the beginning before we began intercession, I got up and told the church members to pray for me that I knew I had been possessed by an evil spirit. The members never asked questions. If you say you have a problem, they begin to intercede immediately. They got up and headed towards me and immediately I fell to the floor. While they were praying for me that spirit fought hard not to release me. As I laid there on the floor my hands were in a tight clench and the members were trying to separate my arms and whatever it was that had me bound refused to let go. But after much praying and interceding my arms were pried opened and I found some release but not complete and I knew that something else was wrong. I was being drained of my spiritual life, and this I was not going to tolerate.

I had just returned a few weeks earlier from visiting my sister in Florida. I made the trip with my youngest sister (who was in remission from breast cancer and I thought it would be a good idea to bring her with me) so that she can see the family. The reason I mention this particular trip is because I thought that I had brought back this evil spirit with me from Florida. I had to find the cause of my change. There was a denial on my part that it could not be me who actually possessed this evil spirit. I needed to blame someone else.

"Turn away from evil and do good. Search for peace, and work to maintain it." Psalm 34:14 (NLT)

My fourth year of marriage was a very tumultuous year for me, and there was "no holds bar" when it came to telling each other what we felt about one another. For example, he would tell me my faults and I would tell him his and it would turn into a shouting match. We went as far as telling each other what a mistake it was to have married but neither one of us was willing to go for a divorce.

He told me that he would not divorce me because our marriage had been God-ordained. I agreed maybe God did send him to me on that day to fix the roof of the property and maybe I was to invite him to church and maybe he would have given his life to Christ, but I think that I was to be a friend and nothing more. But like a fool I allowed myself to be enticed by this younger man with a business who found me attractive enough to ask me out, how little did I think of myself. So, to keep my sanity I decided to think of C as a vacationing partner. But I was still expected to comply with my wifely duties.

Truth be told, when I began to look at him as a partner of sorts, I was able to tolerate him. I also noticed something that I had overlooked before and that is while we were both on vacation, he was a totally different person. His attitude and behavior was not that bad, and I start to enjoy his company more when we were away from the home environment. I learned to tune out the bad things going on in my relationship and enjoy the trips. But I knew that this was not right since I did not love him like a woman in love should love a man, I loved him for his generosity and I knew to be kind to him because I could not hate him, it was not Christ-like. I wanted to keep the peace between us as much as possible. I had given up arguing and fighting with anyone many years ago.

FATHER GRANT ME YOUR PEACE

You will keep in perfect peace all who trust in you, all whose thoughts are fixed on you! Isaiah 26:3 (NLT)

Many years before I met him I had made up my mind to seek peace and to be at peace with everyone. I would tell him how inappropriate it was for him to be constantly arguing the way he did, when he professed being a Christian. All I wanted was to have peace in my life and with C in my life it was highly unlikely because my discussions with him were pertinent to my stability, the one that I had become accustomed to for years before I met him. He considered my discussions arguments and nagging when I raised the issues about his spending, and lack of communication about important decisions. However, I made sure that no one outside of us was aware of the issues we were experiencing. We continued to attend church with all smiles and hugs. Going to events together with other church members and everyone thinks that we are the most handsome couple in the church and most in-love couple there, but it is all a façade.

I had difficulty finding peace within myself. I began to notice that I was becoming more and more emotionally and mentally sick because of the constant arguing. And my sleepless nights did not help me at all because I felt like something was always trying to squeeze my heart out.

I had to pray every night for God to guard my heart because I would wake up in the middle of the night with pain in my heart. I realized after a while that every time I slept in the same bed even when we went on vacation that I had to pray to God to guard my heart or else I would not be able to sleep through the night. I knew that it was not this man sleeping next to me that was reaching over to hurt me but something else.

CHAPTER 32

MERCY

"Once you were dead because of your disobedience and your many sins. You used to live in sin, just like the rest of the world, obeying the devil—the commander of the powers in the unseen world. He is the spirit at work in the hearts of those who refuse to obey God. All of us used to live that way, following the passionate desires and inclinations of our sinful nature. By our very nature we were subject to God's anger, just like everyone else. But God is so rich in mercy, and he loved us so much, that even though we were dead because of our sins, he gave us life when he raised Christ from the dead. It is only by God's grace that you have been saved!"

Ephesians 2:1-5 (NLT)

LIBERATION

I knew I had to make the decision to separate myself from the marriage. I had already begged God to forgive me for my disobedience and rebellion. I also had to pray hard and long for God's guidance. God in His infinite mercy granted me an opportunity to be released from what had me bound.

It was on a Sunday afternoon that I was given the opportunity to demonstrate my true repentance in the presence of other saints. C called me after church that Sunday to invite me to go with him to a birthday party. One of the members from his church had invited him over to his brother's home to celebrate his birthday. The house was full of the birthday guy's family, friends and other church members. God would use this time where there were other believers present to manifest his power over the enemy.

I ran into an old friend there, who happened to be a pastor and was pastoring his own church at the time. He was a security officer at the agency where I worked and his wife worked in medical records. We had become good friends throughout the years that we worked together.

They both enjoyed singing and had recorded a gospel music album some years earlier. Anyhow, the house was full with people and everyone was talking and having a good time. The hostess, a very spiritual woman I'm told, called out to her sister-in-law and began to pray over her and to prophesy to her.

After that, she began to call others to pray over them, and then she called me. She turned and prayed for me and as she was praying, I fell to the floor and the voice in me began to rebuke Satan in a loud voice. I had no control of my body or speech at that point. The others who were there began to intercede and help me rebuke Satan. Everyone surrounded me and they all began to pray for me and to ask that spirit that was in me to lose me and come out of me and I just kept on repeating these words, "I rebuke you Satan, I rebuke you Satan" until I felt a peace overcome me.

In my life I had to contend with evil spirits but never in my Christian life had I had to contend with an evil spirit as strong as this one. I believe that on that day, God had called His army of warriors to assemble in that house to contend with what had me bound for those five years. As I look back to that day, I remember that everyone in that home (I can say with certainty) were true believers of the word of God and served the Lord with all of their heart, soul, and mind. I believe that the angels of the Lord were there in full force and I do believe that it was no coincidence. I believe in my heart that God had orchestrated the entire event and to Him be the glory. Because on that day I felt that I was fully liberated from the stronghold that Satan had on me. I saw the importance of being surrounded by the servants of the Lord because the angels of God are there watching after each and every one of us. There is victory in numbers and that day it was proof of what a group of Christians can do when they all come together on one accord to pray for one of their own.

DETERMINATION

"I have told you all this so that you may have peace in me. Here on earth you will have many trials and sorrows. But take heart, because I have overcome the world." John 16:33 (NLT)

On New Year's Day 2010, five months earlier, from my liberation experience I had told myself that I would have peace. I told myself that I would not argue with C because I was determined to have peace in my heart, in my mind, and in my soul.

I decided to try something new, a different strategy because I had tried everything else. I had tried therapy both in the secular world and then in Pastoral counseling and none of them did any good. The peace that I so yearned for and worked to achieve when I gave my life to Christ had been sapped but I was going to change it around. I had decided to move to the spare room of the duplex. It was the computer and office space, and it had a futon that I cushioned it with a foam mattress and I slept there for that year. I did not feel anyone squeezing my heart and I slept better than I had slept in years, to God be the glory.

CHAPTER 33

I STILL HAVE A PURPOSE IN LIFE

For he has rescued us from the kingdom of darkness and transferred us into the Kingdom of his dear Son, who purchased our freedom and forgave our sins. Colossians 1:13-14 (NLT)

GOD MAKES THE GLUE

That decision to ignore the voice of God will resonate in me until the day that I die. Every decision that I made without going to God in prayer had traumatic consequences. As I recount the last several years from the time that I widowed to the time that I got married to C to the time that I walked away from my marriage, the one thing that sticks out the most are the decisions that I made without the counsel of God. Can I speak to God and expect an answer? Absolutely! But I found that out a little too late because of my impatience. But thank God for His infinite mercy and grace. It was this same God that loved me so much that He called me to serve Him and only Him would be the same God that I would turn my back on in a moment of human weakness.

I turned my anger toward this same loving God because I stupidly and foolishly blamed Him for allowing my husband to die and not revive him. I would later discover what the impact of having chosen sin over God would have on my spiritual life, my family, my physical body and my mental health. I had lost my properties, my children were scattered and they became estranged from each other. I lost the respect of my children and grandchildren.

My H was the glue that held the family together but God is the maker of the glue that will hold us together again. I felt that I had completely lost my true purpose in life, but for the grace of God.

GODLY WISDOM HELPS

I should have kept in mind that on my strength, I couldn't have done anything. I made the decision to stop mourning the death of my beloved husband and gave up on the grieving process was not a wise choice. That choice catapulted me into my next decision of requesting another companion without waiting for God to reveal to me my purpose for his Kingdom.

I then decided to open a business without putting it in prayer before the Lord. I made the decision to pay for it with credit cards, which was a bad decision that eventually landed me in debt. The decision to get married to someone I didn't love was ungodly. To pay for the entire wedding with my savings and borrow $5,000 from the bank was ludicrous. To give my home of twenty years to a stranger to rent was nothing short of the greed for money, and that's why I lost it.

The zaniest yet was to buy the three family property on Fairfield avenue was not what God had in mind for me. I had been warned against buying it by a friend in the faith and I did not listen to him. The decision to leave my church home and go to a church elsewhere was not in God's plan either. The last and final decision resulted the most painful for me in the end which was to move away from my beloved children and grandchildren. That was very devastating to say the least.

But through it all, God never left me, and He never forsook me, even when I did not want to listen to His voice he knew that I still loved Him so. I know in my heart that God still has something greater for me, even if it doesn't include a husband.

I still can't fathom the stronghold I was under. I had the funds in my 401K to leave the marriage at any time but something more powerful than me kept me in that marriage.

That marriage had been the distraction that kept me from following my calling. I never knew that I could despise life so much when I was living in that situation.

THERE IS NO HATE IN GOD'S KINGDOM

Yet I did not know why I should have hated that situation and despised the marriage so much when it was all my entire fault. Except that it was me, in my sub-conscience that I was hating. But that was the kind of dilemma I found myself in. I realize the importance of knowing the voice of God and taking heed to it. Never take God for granted. When he tells you to flee he means it, RUN!

Living that deceptive life started to take a toll on my spiritual life and I knew that I was sinning and that it was wrong and I really did not want to do it. I had become deceitful and that was not who I was. I didn't recognize that person. At that time, since I did not see a way out of my situation all I could do to keep my sanity was to treat myself to trips. I would tell myself that since I was stuck in the marriage that I might as well learn to love him, but I did not want to love him. I hated that I had lost everything that my late husband and I had worked so hard to achieve. I felt so ashamed of myself. I hated where I was from where I had been seven years before I married. I just could not stand myself living in that marriage because as long as I was there, I could not forgive myself and would always remember what a fool I had been.

I gave this marriage all the energy that I had so I had refused to be the only one trying to hold something together that was destined to fail in the long run. I thought that if it's not from God don't bother to salvage it.

One of my female friends had tried to tell me what a mistake I was making but it was not until after several years that she said to me, there was just no way to reach you because you were on a rollercoaster and you didn't want anyone to bring you down from it. A couple that knew me and my late husband for over twenty-five years had interviewed C indiscreetly and had given me the "green light," because he appeared to be a good man was what my friend told me. My daughter didn't know what to say about my decision because she was going through some things in her own marriage. She didn't quite clue me on what was happening in her home so I thought she was handling it. But I found out later and she had accused me of not being there for her during her situation. I was so blind to everything that was going on around me and all I thought about was that I was doing the right thing for me and my family. I will have to bear that pain for the rest of my life. Rejecting God is an awful offense, especially for a Christian because nothing good can come out of it.

"It would be better if they had never known the way to righteousness than to know it and then reject the command they were given to live a holy life."
2 Peter 2:21 (NLT)

GOD EXPECTS CIVILITY AMONG HIS CHILDREN

I had decided to reconcile myself to God and start a new year concentrating on my spiritual life and change my ways in a way that would please God. I decided to stop arguing and learn to love C like a brother in the faith and not expect too much from him and just live my life according to God's will. I prayed to God to release me from the grips of the devil that had me bound and to free me to move away for the sake of both C and my spiritual life.

I remained civil and we both knew and understood that it was for the best and he agreed that my moving away and taking time away would do me some good. He thought that this was a temporary move that I was making and I had explained to him many times before that I would not be returning but he had refused to listen to what I would tell him so I would leave it at that to avoid arguments.

We continued to stay in touch with each other and being the person that he is he would bail me out of financial situations whenever I called him. I would offer to pay him back every dollar, but of course he would not take it. I had to move eighteen hundred miles away so that I would not have to pay off the cash loans in sexual favors, I had begun to get sick of doing that and I felt very much like a woman selling her body for money, even if he was my husband.

WHAT'S THE POINT OF REGRETS?

Things would had been much better for me if I had been able to move back to my home in Stratford where I lived in before I got married and then none of what happened for the five years would have happened to me.

I would had live a different life. I would still be there and my children would still be visiting me and having Sunday dinners. If only my ex-brother-in-law were different and I would've been able to get back to my home, then I would have had the marriage annulled. I know that I shouldn't dwell on what I had lost in terms of material things but I had so many memories in that home that I had accumulated throughout the twenty-one years that I lived there. I had to get rid of most of it. I had to give away many things that I was saving for my children and grandchildren.

There were so many photos ruined of my family due to the poor storage areas and not to mention the books that I had purchased over the years—especially the Encyclopedia Britannica that my late husband had bought for our youngest son when he was two years old. When my youngest son asked me about it, I felt so bad when I had to tell him that it was ruined in the storage area in the garage and I had to throw it away. I lost some very precious memories such as trinkets and souvenirs that I had saved from our many vacations together when my children were younger. It was a major mistake that will always come to mind to hurt me but I will allow it to come in and go out the same way. It will be just a passing thought that I will not let consume me anymore.

I started to attend my old church on Sunday evenings and on Wednesday nights looking to get fed by the word ministered there. By that time my old Pastor had died of a heart attack and I was so hurt by that loss that it upset me because he was supposed to be my mentor. I'm at a crossroad there not knowing and not very sure about my ministry. Now I'm hopefully looking to see if anyone there could help me find my ministry. I had set in my mind that I would live in harmony with Him and I did just that

CHANGE IS GOOD

I walked away from the marriage on April 1st of 2011, one month after our sixth year anniversary. I moved to my own apartment some 40 minutes away.

I moved to this extremely quiet neighborhood in a four room apartment that was more like a matchbox. It was that small and it was on the second floor of a three family dwelling. I liked it because it was all mine and there was no one to take my peace but I was lonely for my family and friends. The reason I took it was two-fold. I wanted to live in peace, and because I had just relocated to a new position within my job and was sent to another town and it was only 15 minutes away from my new apartment.

I did not care much for the new area although I did feel some sense of peace there. I was eventually out of the home but not free completely because I continued to invite him over and relied on him for funds. In some strange way I actually missed him when I was distanced from him and wanted to stay friends. I didn't feel any animosity toward him, that would be ungodly anyway.

I had decided to move to San Antonio Texas after much prayer and supplication to God, and He granted my prayer and gave me permission to move, the following year. I had put in my papers to take an early retirement. I retired from my job after twenty years and was thinking of going into the education field. I had in mind to attend Cornerstone church in San Antonio whose Pastors are John Hagee and Matthew Hagee.

However, even, after my separation from C, we became travelling partners if nothing else, and he would always take care of the expenses. We are not divorced as of the writing of this book and continue to stay in touch with each other, although I live in another state, eighteen hundred miles away.

In the end, I realized something about C and he deserves recognition for this and that is his kind heart and generous spirit. Through this experience, I learned the lesson that I don't have the power to change people. I didn't understand that of him which caused many of the issues in our marriage but I understand now he is who he is and no one can change that; and why would anyone want to. He isn't the only one wired that way. I'm living by myself depending on God to meet all of my needs and C still calls me to ask if I need something and being who he is, helps me with funds to compensate my income.

NO POINTING FINGERS PLEASE!

I had to blame someone throughout my marriage and so I began to blame C for all of my misfortunes. I wanted to repress the real truth. I wanted to look at things from a totally different perspective. So, it was all his fault and I was the victim who fell prey to his lies. Although, he was not without fault and he had given me enough reasons to mistrust him and think the worse of him. Yes, I had decided to put most of the blame on him for some of the things that went wrong in my life and this marriage. I did not know it then as I know it now, if anyone made me lose everything; family, friends, and property I'd have to blame myself because of my disobedience to God compounded by my foolish decisions.

CHAPTER 24

SPIRITUAL AWAKENING

"The Spirit of the LORD is upon me, for he has anointed me to bring Good News to the poor. He has sent me to proclaim that captives will be released, that the blind will see that the oppressed will be set free, and that the time of the LORD's favor has come." Luke 4:18-19 (NLT)

A LOVING SAVIOR

But, for the grace of God I would eventually be made whole again as God would begin to make me spiritually aware and supernaturally, how to recognize the ways Satan deceives his prey, the way he had deceived me. God showed me how I had allowed Satan to enter my life and my home. It took me five long years to be free from the grips of the devil and I did not do it on my own but with the help of my heavenly Father, the one who loves me, forever. Inspired by God, I had to learn and know how the devil worked and about his tactics in order to know how to defeat him and how I had to arm myself and get away from his diabolical scheme to destroy me. God gave me the spiritual tools that I needed and I listened to him that time. I know that my life would never be the same after what I experienced but I never stopped believing in the one and true God, so I survived Satan's deception and his attacks to steal my life and rob me of everything that was precious to me. By the grace of God who is my loving Savior, I kept the faith and hope for a better future. As long as I had hope, even when I did not consult with God on my decisions, He was always faithful and I knew that His "mercies endured forever.

I am my new found home in San Antonio, Texas. I am living in a two-bedroom apartment receiving a monthly State

Retirement Pension check, estranged from my family and everyone I know because of the foolish decisions I made eleven years ago.

I moved to get away from the nightmare, escape the demons that had been tormenting me over the mistakes I had made. Such as, my past sexual weaknesses, the stupidity of believing Satan's lies, the guilt of losing the properties that H had left me and squandering away the life insurance money; and especially losing what was most precious to me, the love of my beloved children and grandchildren. How I ached to be with my children and grandchildren. I moved away from the people I loved the most and I missed them tremendously.

THE TRUTH REVEALED

One night as I began to have those disturbing guilt-filled and shameful thoughts and I'm crying out in anguish, the Spirit of the Lord revealed to me that Satan had meant to stop what God had called me to do and I immediately felt a sense of peace fall over me and I felt led by the spirit to sit in front of the computer and I just began to write what the spirit had lead me to write. I gave into the Spirit and through the direction of the Holy Spirit I began to write the following:

"Satan had meant to stop you from doing what God had called you to do for His Kingdom and that your husband [his death] was the instrument Satan used to stop that work. And, that since I was a widow and vulnerable that I would be susceptible to any man's enticement and seduction."

I kept on writing as I was lead to write and I cried and cried, and cried until I was drinking my tears and the mucus kept filling my nasal passage and rolling out of my nose.

"The devil knew her weaknesses and how angry she was at God. So he took advantage of her. The work that God had for her in the north east was big where many souls would have been saved by her evangelism. She was to work closely

with Bishop and become a minister of good will and go into the streets and evangelize [to] the lost souls. The East south end of this major city in the northeast that had many a population of lost souls that were in need of God and the harvest was ready. The Bishop was to prepare her for this gathering of souls but she was taken away at her prime. She needed all of her attention on the kingdom of God and there was to be no distractions. Her husband was ready to go to his home in heaven I could have kept him longer but he wanted, he wanted to come home and he knew that God would take care of her. The devil knew that she would take sex over you (God) because she was angry at God for taking her husband. She wanted a Christian man but that would have been too easy she would have done everything that God had wanted her to do. But Satan needed her to choose someone that would not be that invested in God's Kingdom. Satan gave her eyes for property and business and vacations and glamorous clothes and dinners out and jewelry to keep her focus off from the things of God and the real calling on her life. This was what the devil had in store for you but I saw your tears and your true feelings for the kingdom and I saw your heart you loved me more and now I lose you from the evil one you are my daughter forever. Your husband is not the bad guy in the story, neither one of you were, it was Satan and his scheme to destroy you and to destroy what God had put together. This marriage is not dissolved as of yet. But you have work to do for the kingdom of God and that is to keep doing what you are doing."

That night I sat at my computer just writing whatever came to my mind and so I began to put my thoughts on paper. I started writing about my disappointed and unsatisfying life. I had to start from the beginning on how my life changed. For the story to have the validity it has, I had to put C in the person that I saw with my eye lenses and that way you saw what I saw. I did not know that Satan was behind the scenes manipulating me. So I had to blame C for my actions in disobeying God.

My reason for writing my story was because I had received a revelation from God to tell other women about my experience and to discourage them from falling into that same trap that I fell into because of a foolish anger toward God. I am not trying to say that believers can't get angry at God we just have to have discernment when we do it. God should never be blamed for the mess that we create in our lives. I had been disobedient and I allowed Satan to take control of me when I did not listen to the voice of God telling me to flee. God had never forsaken me but He stepped aside when I refused to listen to Him and I rebelled against Him. Sinning is doing anything that displeases God, and it goes against His Biblical teachings. When I had sex with C that night I had fornicated with him and I had sinned against God. And if I had gone home that night and asked God to forgive me and not done it again, God would have forgiven me but when I told God to His face what I told Him that went beyond the scope of a sin because I had allowed the evil one to be my master. I had violated the second of the Ten Commandments:

"Thou shalt have no other gods before me."
Exodus 20:3 (KJV)

Throughout the book, I have shared the many facets of my life and how sin had played a major role in it. Growing up in a home with alcoholic parents and the psychological scars caused by the neglect and abuse left me with a residue of that past life that I had not fully buried and it played a major role that Satan used to take my focus off of my purpose and goal for the Kingdom of God.

TAKE HEED

I was a godly woman. I should never have gone into a single man's bedroom and let alone lie on his bed. Godly women who are seeking a husband, the bedroom is not where they should look. The search starts with prayer and supplications and believing that God would find them their helpmate.

Do not give God specifications. The focus should be on God and His Kingdom. God wants a spouse that will treat his children with respect. Including God in all of our decision making is crucial. Satan is not a gentleman and he sits around waiting especially when we are in our most vulnerable and in our weakest state.

I give God all the glory because my conscience would no longer hold me captive nor in bondage. I have been made free forever of my guilt and shame. And, all those years that were stolen from me and everything that I lost, will be restored to me again. In Psalm 32:5 I have God's promise in that if, *"Finally, I confessed all my sins to you and stopped trying to hide my guilt. I said to myself, "I will confess my rebellion to the LORD." And you forgave me! All my guilt is gone."* NLT

So don't lose hope. There is a better tomorrow if you believe. But at last, I was inspired in my heart that forgiveness toward others and myself, especially forgiving myself was the beginning. Romans 8:1, *"Therefore there is no condemnation for those who are in Christ Jesus, who live, walk not after the dictates of the flesh, but after the dictates of the Spirit."* (NLT)

I thought that if I wrote what I had been through for those years, I would receive the long awaited liberation from the torment of my past. *"For You oh Lord, are good, and ready to forgive; and You are abundant in mercy and loving-kindness to all who call upon You"* Psalm 86:5 (NLT). My conscience would no longer hold me captive nor in bondage. AMEN!

CHAPTER 35

HOPE

"So many are saying, "God will never rescue him!" But you, O LORD, are a shield around me; you are my glory, the one who holds my head high. I cried out to the LORD, and he answered me from his holy mountain. I lay down and slept, yet I woke up in safety, for the LORD was watching over me. I am not afraid of ten thousand enemies who surround me on every side." Psalm 3:2-6 (NLT)

FROM A DARK PLACE INTO THE LIGHT

Two years had passed since I started writing my story. This particular night, I'm sitting in front of the computer still somewhat upset at the ways things had turned out and anger and rage swelled up in me. I began to write this vision that I had received at that moment. I had no idea where it came from because I wasn't even thinking along those lines.

In the vision I am entering a tunnel sitting inside a horse-driven carriage, (sort of like a carriage used in a "Cinderella" story) with two men standing in the back of the carriage and two men sitting in front of it. They are all dressed in what appeared to be colonial clothing, they had the white ruffled shirts under the lace embroidered wide-collared waistcoats and knee-length breeches. As we travel through the tunnel it began to get narrower towards the exit and then somewhere along the way I am no longer sitting in the carriage but it seems that we have left the horse and carriage behind. The men and I continue to walk forward to what appears to be the exit but we are force to crawl on our knees in this dark tunnel as it is getting smaller and smaller (something out of "Alice in Wonderland"). We are about to go down on our knees; then it is pitch black and I can feel the dirt underneath me and on my hands. At that moment I am afraid and I'm getting dirty. I hate the dirt! I continue to crawl. I don't know what happened to the other two men. I see a small hole in front of me that appears to be coming from above, meaning I am under the ground. Buried. I am trying to get out through this small opening. I come out of that hole and find myself all alone in what appears to be a spacious forest that is wide and unending with trees that stretch up high into the heavens. All I could see of the trees are the huge brown trunks not the branches nor the leaves and as I look across, the tree trunks disappear and I am surrounded by beautiful luscious green grass that goes on forever; and I look up to the sky and I see a beautiful clear bright blue sky with no clouds in sight. I find myself in this beautiful place completely alone, the carriage drivers and horses have disappeared and I do not know where I am, and I'm afraid. The vision ends there.

I could see how I was in a dark place that felt like I was buried alive. But coming out of that dark and awful place into the beautiful light even if I was alone, I'm alive and God is with me and He will give me a new beginning. That's how I perceived that vision.

I'M HOPEFUL

Even when I was filled with fear, I still had hope, I knew that I was not alone in this world. God had been with me all along and He would continue to be with me no matter what the circumstances. God's revelation made me realized one thing that my conscience would no longer hold me captive nor in bondage. I would eventually be free of my guilt and shame, and that all those years that were stolen from me and everything that I lost would be restored to me. So don't lose hope, there is a better tomorrow if you believe. You have read my story I pray that you will be encouraged and remain hopeful. Because the God that I serve is the God who can "set the captives free," and you too can be liberated and restored.

"For the Lord is the Spirit, and wherever the Spirit of the Lord is, there is freedom." 2 Corinthians 3:17 (NLT)

I could not forgive myself, for in my mind I had messed up everything and didn't deserve to be forgiven. I was inspired to forgive. Forgiveness is the beginning of peace. I wrote to be liberated. I can now walk tall with confidence that no matter what may come my way God will fight my battles and I will be victorious. My conscience would no longer hold me captive nor in bondage. I believed that all those years that were stolen from me and everything that I lost would be restored to me again.

CHAPTER 36

HUMAN MISTAKES...
GODLY RESPONSES

"Yes, it is good to abstain from sexual relations. But because there is so much sexual immorality, each man should have his own wife, and each woman should have her own husband. The husband should fulfill his wife's sexual needs, and the wife should fulfill her husband's needs. The wife gives authority over her body to her husband, and the husband gives authority over his body to his wife. Do not deprive each other of sexual relations, unless you both agree to refrain from sexual intimacy for a limited time so you can give yourselves more completely to prayer. Afterward, you should come together again so that Satan won't be able to tempt you because of your lack of self-control."

1 Corinthians 7:1-5 (NLT)

MARRIAGE AND FAMILY

I am not a "Marriage and Family" therapist nor an expert to talk to anyone about such matters but I share my story in faith that my experience will be a beacon to those going through some similar issues and who have concerns about their own relationships.

My hope is that it may help you to understand that just because we serve a righteous and just God, we are not exempt us from making mistakes and creating chaos in our Christian walk. We live and learn. But we must understand that there will be consequences when we ignore God's warnings through not knowing his voice or because we choose to do it our way. I strongly believe that the mistakes I made were in part, if not entirely, due to my disobedience to the voice of God.

My first mistake was thinking that I was invincible in not allowing myself to feel the death of my late husband and pretend that I was alright before my family and everyone else. I regretted not having had that experience of grieving out loud where everyone would have known my true pain and suffering. Why did I think that I had to pretend I did not need someone to comfort me? I realized later that it was alright to have been more vocal and allow them to call me and come over to comfort me. Instead, I refused to allow anyone to see my frail side. It was very wrong of me to prevent my children and grandchildren from seeing the real person and allowing them to grieve with me as well. I deprived them of suffering alongside me. It was a lonely time for me and it did not have to be. Again why did I have to take the drug Xanax, which prevented me from feeling? Instead, that drug kept me numb and too relaxed. I could not even shed a tear nor show any kind of emotion. It was not fair to my daughter because I could not even comfort nor console her during that tragic time in her life. That was the only father figure she ever knew.

If you ever have to go through such an experience, seek God and counseling if you must, but by all means, ball your eyes out cry and go through the true grieving process, of anger, denial, acceptance, and letting go (I got this tidbit from the Kubler-Ross model on the grieving process.) But when I did not do that there was unfinished business that lingered on for a long time and it did a terrible job on my mind. Perhaps if I had allowed myself to properly grieve I would have done it for the length I needed to and not put stipulations on God. And if I had just left well enough alone, my life might have gone different direction. Maybe avoiding the mess that I created in life. Imagine that, me telling God what was best for me, what a joke and it all backfired on me big time.

I know now that there is a reason why people must take their time with the grieving process and just let it all take its course and allow God to do the rest. How different things would had been for me and my family, I know this now, but it is never too late with God on my side.

My second mistake was ignoring my family who were also grieving and thinking that they were alright just because I was pretending that I was alright. Who gave me the right to stop them from their grieving process. It was as if they were not permitted to show any kind of emotions that indicated that they were suffering the loss of their father or for their grandfather.

Jesus cried for Lazarus, and the people saw and said, "see how much he loved him!" John 11:35-36 (NLT)

When we take our eyes off of God, we become dependent on our own strength; what a huge mistake. We don't know how to work out situations in our lives so we tend to get lost in the midst of things. Allow yourself to be vulnerable and allow others to see your weaknesses because you never know if God has put them there to strengthen you. We are nothing but mere humans and have many flaws and when we try to hide them from others, we make a mistake because we are robbing them of their blessings. They have been placed there strategically by God and are there waiting to bless us during our most difficult time. God will use anyone.

My third mistake was rushing into a marriage with someone just because I had sex with him. Women should be very aware and take their time to explore each other's needs, desires, and wants because we all have different ways of looking at things in our own lives. Seek God first which is what I did not do directly. Look to know each other's intimate desires through verbalizing them and not by expressions. Wait until the honeymoon. Be aware of the weakness of your flesh. Just because we are Christian adults doesn't make us except from having human emotions and desires. So stay away from each other for some time if the feelings are too strong. But do not by any form or fashion temp each other. The tempter, Satan is looking for the smallest physical contact, but wait until the wedding day.

The devil is the biggest deceiver and tempter and if you touch one another, you are human and have emotions and feelings and you alone will not be able to contain the desire to engage in sex. Kudos to those who are able to resist. The best thing to do is to wait until your wedding day and your marriage bed.

My fourth mistake was trusting. Just because someone tells you that they go church doesn't mean you can believe everything they tell you. Although he meant well and I can't fault him entirely. I was totally the blame for how my life turned out. Do not ever blame anyone for your shortcomings, they are yours and you own them. Everything that you do, you do by choice. Whatever happens or whatever the consequences are, they are all brought on by your decisions. Yes, Satan will come to you and make you do things that you are not aware that you're doing, there is no question about it. But ultimately it's how we respond to all the situations in our life and how strong our walk with the Lord is that will help us endure.

"Where he was tempted by the devil for forty days. Jesus ate nothing all that time and became very hungry" Luke 4:2 (NLT). Jesus' response to the devil was to quote the scripture. Be very aware of Satan's tactics because he knows who you are and your weaknesses. Satan attends church along with the rest of us.

Learn to trust each other and be very honest with one another, you don't have to go into your past lives but tell each other everything about your present and what you are doing in the here and now. Do not hide anything from one another. Tell each other about your fears and concerns and worries, be very honest. And never give the devil, the deceiver a foothold nor open the door for him to come in and create chaos in your courtship nor in your marriage.

"Love is patient and kind. Love is not jealous or boastful or proud [5] or rude. It does not demand its own way. It is not irritable, and it keeps no record of being wronged. [6] It does not rejoice about injustice but rejoices whenever the truth wins out. [7] Love never gives up, never loses faith, is always hopeful, and endures through every circumstance."

1 Corinthians 13:4-7 (NLT)

My fifth mistake was believing that I could conjure up love for C out of the air. That I would teach him how to love me in return. Love is not taught. We either love or we don't but there is no in between. Again, I'm not an expert I am only speaking from my experience. I loved H with all my heart and I didn't want to love anyone else. I never should had gotten remarried. I couldn't love C because first I had to love myself. I hated what I had become and I loathed my very existence. It wasn't him who I was despising it was me.

Never get tired of your life. It is a gift from God. Be kind to one another and love each other with every ounce of your being. Never ever stop enjoying each other's company. Always treat each other like first time lovers and be seductive to one another after you are married. That way you will keep the marriage alive and well. Even after you have children, don't stop having intimate moments and dates with one another. Let the children know that mom and dad belong to one another just as children belong to them. That way the children will see that behavior in the home and will learn how to be that way with their future spouses and children.

My hope and prayer is that in some way, generations will live happy and joyful lives and that the divorce rates will dramatically decrease if the human race can let and allow God to guide and instruct us in the way that we should go. I read this book that goes by the title, "Let Go," by Fenelon. One of my former colleagues and I were having a discussion about the subject of letting go of things in our lives and allowing God to give us the direction we need. He told me about this book. I ordered it online through Amazon.com and paid about three dollars for it. In the book, there is a quote by Henry Van Dyke, who said "Self is the only prison that can bind the soul." How very true is that statement.

As Christians we are our own worst enemy. In the introduction of the same book Robert Whitaker, President of Whitaker House Publishing, states that, "Every Christian who is really serious about living the Christ-like life craves freedom from bondage. The intensity of the struggle which goes on in the hearts of countless Christians gives testimony to the great need for us to learn to let go of our selfish, sinful lives to become the new creations Jesus meant us to be." (1973)

PUT ON THE WHOLE ARMOR...

"Put on all of God's armor so that you will be able to stand firm against all strategies of the devil. For we are not fighting against flesh-and-blood enemies, but against evil rulers and authorities of the unseen world, against mighty powers in this dark world, and against evil spirits in the heavenly places. Therefore, put on every piece of God's armor so you will be able to resist the enemy in the time of evil. Then after the battle you will still be standing firm." Ephesians 6:11-18 (NLT)

My struggle was not with "flesh and blood" but "spiritual forces" that were beyond my control because I let down my guard. It was during my weakest moment that Satan and his demons would have their way with me and begin to influence my every thought. The Bible had the answer to all my woes, I just didn't take heed. I understand the importance of what it means to put on the whole armor of God.

Our marriage was doomed for failure from the very beginning because it had not been blessed by God. God had already revealed to me to get away from him. God knew that it would be a disaster and He wanted to save us both all the pain and disappointments. God knows best.

I really thought that C had been sent by God to rescue me from my pain and suffering that he was my blessing from above. I began to look at myself differently in that although I had a college degree there was no reason why I could not marry someone without a degree. I began to have these thoughts about helping him be more ambitious and grow his business into a huge conglomerate, and perhaps he would go back to school to get a degree in business, like H.

Satan would use our most vulnerable times in our lives to plant seeds of doubt about God's love and seeds of lies about how God will failed us. In a weakened state of mind, we might believe the lies of the devil and developed an attitude toward God. I began to trust more in myself and in my decisions than in God. For five years, I would be barren, unable to birth what God had impregnated me with, the spirit of evangelism. I had been saved by grace to serve the Lord and I thought that I was a mature Christian but I was put out of commission in my prime.

CHAPTER 37

I AM A CHILD OF GOD

"But you belong to God, my dear children. You have already won a victory over those people, because the Spirit who lives in you is greater than the spirit who lives in the world" 1 John 4:4, NLT

YOUR WILL BE DONE...

My calling in life is to ascribe to whatever the Lord God requests of me. I learned something else and that is that I am no longer afraid of the present circumstances when it all looks like everything is going haywire nor of what the future holds because I know that I know that God has it all under His control and I will not fear.

I thank God for his amazing grace and His forgiving power. I can now walk tall with confidence that no matter what may come my way, God will fight my battles and I will be victorious. I can say now with certainty that I am a child of God and that nothing and no one will be able to ever sway me from serving God and following His calling in my life.

Satan might have thought that he had me but God can take a bad situation and turn it around for good. God can still use me. God's plan for my life is not over until He says it's over.

I will keep doing what He had asked me to do for His glory and honor. I am no longer my own, I never was, and I have been bought with a price Jesus Christ died that I may live. He was buried so that my sins will be forgiven, and He rose again on the third day so that I may have life and that more abundantly and forever more. I had made my peace with God and He was gracious to receive me back to Him for God is still my shield and protector. Psalm 18:2 lets me know that, *"The Lord is my rock, my fortress, and my Savior; my God is my rock, in whom I find protection. He is my shield, the power that saves me, and my place of safety."* (NLT)

God continues to love me through all that mess. He waited for me to call Him, really call Him and say to Him I have had enough of this madness. I need you to come get me out of here and out of all this mess, please God, and He did.

Addendum

By the time this book had gone into publication I had been divorced a year and 11 months. We have remained friends. He would still invite me out to dinner with the expectation that we'd get back together. We have tried to spark some new romance between us but it has not worked because I can't seem to love him as he should be loved. He was very instrumental in moving me back to Connecticut and I will always appreciate him for that, as well as be grateful to him for going out of his way. I encouraged him to date other women and I pray that he will find true love one day soon.

I have to say that my daughter and I have reconciled and we are taking one day at a time. We will make new memories from this day forward. I am closer to my sons and grand-children and great-grandchildren. I thank God for giving me long life to be a great-grandmother. My family knows where I live and they are welcome to visit as much as they want, it would be just fine with me. I had the opportunity to spend a weekend with my daughter and three of her daughters in Newport Rhode Island and I could not ask for anything more.

I know that in the times we live in everyone gets busy and we should not expect that our family members will be around us all the time. But for me just being in the same state and especially within a few miles from them makes me happy. My daughter and I have decided that we would get together at least once a month and have a girl's day or night out, and a family dinner every three to four months and I'm good with that. I see them more often than when I was in Texas. I love each one with all my heart. God is a Rewarder of those who diligently seek Him and He has not forgotten His promises.

"And it is impossible to please God without faith. Anyone who wants to come to Him must believe that God exists and that He rewards those who sincerely seek Him." Hebrews 11:6. (NLT)

I received my recompense. It was a tough journey trying to get money back from the contractors but my lawyer worked as hard as she could to get me something for my loss. I was in such debt that when I received my first check it had to go toward my outstanding debt and it helped a little bit I have to say.

Then one day when I thought that all was lost, I received another check and that also went toward other debts. But I was not out of the woods yet because I had accumulated so much debt that it didn't quite make a dent in all that I owed. Finally, after eight years of waiting to be debt free, I received a check that had nothing to do with the property or the contractors but from an accident claim.

I had a car accident back in May of 2012 only two months before retiring and moving to Texas. My car was hit from behind and I suffered backlash and my sciatic nerve was affected. It took my lawyer four years and two depositions but God was faithful. I had prayed to God for a certain amount that would help me pay off my entire debt and be able to tithe from that money.

When the lawyer asked me to come to his office to sign the final papers I was excited because I knew that God had done the impossible, I felt it in my soul. I was all smiles when the lawyer approached me in the waiting room. I looked at the check and it was exactly the amount I had asked God for. God is the God of the impossible and he will restore to His children what the devil has stolen.

I have been made whole. The problems of this world will not affect me as much anymore. I have God the Father, the Son and the Holy Spirit to guide me. God knows the way I should take.

I would like to end my story with this excerpt from Dr. H. Cloud's book, *The Law of Happiness, How Spiritual Wisdom and*

Modern Science Can Change Your Life; P.17, ¶ 2. "When we are not eating the fruits of the good life that God has created and think that we know what is going to satisfy us instead, we will continue to go hungry. Unsatisfied. Unhappy. Unfulfilled. But because we do not see how we get seduced into thinking the human race can play God and figure it out on our own, we continue to not see the trees with the good fruit that are available right in front of us."

"So I will restore to you the years that the swarming locust has eaten, the crawling locust, the consuming locust, and the chewing locust, My great army which I sent among you. You shall eat in plenty and be satisfied, and praise the name of the LORD your God. Who has dealt wondrously with you; and My people shall never be put to shame."

Joel 2:25-32 (NLT)

References

Ackerman, D. (2007). *The Zookeeper's Wife: A War Story.* Published by W.W. Norton & Company

Anderson, J. (1999). *A Year By The Sea.* DoubleDay, a division of Random House, Inc.

Anderson, J. (2002). *An Unfinished Marriage.* Broadway Books, a division of Random House Publications
Bandele, A. (2009). *Something Like Beautiful.* Published by Harper Collins

Bell, L. (2010). *Claiming Ground.* Alfred Knopf, New York, a division of Random House Publishing

Bridges, J. (2007). *Respectable Sins: Confronting The Sins We Tolerate.* Published by NAVPress

Cisneros, S. (1991). *The House on Mango Street.* Bloomsbury Publishing.

Dr. Cloud, H. (2011). *The Law of Happiness, How Spiritual Wisdom and Modern Science Can Change Your Life.* Howard Books, a division of Simon & Schuster, Inc.

Corvillot, J. (2009). *Family Sentence: The Search for My Cuban-Revolutionary, Prison-Yard, Mystic-hero, Deadbeat Dad.* Published by Beacon Press Books

Dosick, W. (1998). *When Life Hurts.* Harper San Francisco – A Division of Harper/Collins Publications

Eden, D. (2012). *My Peace I leave You: Healing Sexual Wounds with the Help of the Saints.* Ave Maria Press

Fitzgerald, F. S. (1925). *The Great Gatsby*. Charles Scribner's Sons

Forrest, E. (2011). *Your Voice in My Head*, A Memoir. Bloomsbury Publishing

Groom, W. (1986). *Forrest Gump*. Washington Square Press Publications

Haines, C. (2003). *My Mother's Witness: The Peggy Morgan Story*. River City Publishing

Dr. Harley Jr, W. F. (1997). *Your Love & Marriage; Dr. Harley Answers your Personal Questions*. Revell, a division of Baker Publishing Group

Hemingway, E. (1932). *Death In The Afternoon*. Publisher: Charles Scribner's Sons

Kelly, J. (2013. *Etched...Upon My Heart: What We Learn and Why We Never Forget*. Faith Words Publishers

King, S. (2000). *Stephen King On Writing, A Memoir Of The Craft*. Pocket Books, a division of Simon & Schuster, Inc.

Kirshenbaum, M. (1996). *Too Good to Leave, Too Bad to Stay, A Step By Step Guide to Help You Decide Whether to Stay In or Get Out of Your Relationship*. Published by Plume, a division of Penquin Books

Larson, S. (2007). *Alone in Marriage: Encouragement For The Times When It's All Up To You*. Moody Publishers

Lloyd Burns, C. (2006). *It Hit Me Like A Ton of Bricks*. Worth Point Press, a division of Farrar, Strauss, & Giroux

Roiphe, A. (2008). *Epilogue: A Memoir*. Harper Collins Publishers.

ST. Clair, C. (2007). *The Butterfly Garden, A Memoir*. Publisher: Health Communications, Inc.

Steinbeck, J. (1932). *The Pastures of Heaven*. Published by Brewer, Warren, and Putnam

Waller, R. J. (1992). *The Bridges of Madison County*. Warren Books, Inc.

Dr. Ward, W. E. (2011). *The Good Enough Spouse: Resolve or Dissolve Conflicted Marriages*. New Horizon Press, Far Hills New Jersey

Wilson, A. (2010). *When Did I Get Like This?* Harper & Collins Publishers, New York City

Wilson, B. (2006). *The Invisible Bond*. Mulnomah Books Publishing
She speaks to the reader about the impact of sexual bonding

Yerkovich, M. & Yerkovich, K. (2006). *How We Love: Discover Your Love Style, Enhance Your marriage*. Published by Waterbrook, a division of Random House

Kubler-Ross, E. (1969). On Death and Dying: What the dying have to teach doctors, nurse, clergy, and their own families. Published by Scribner

CONTACT THE AUTHOR

www.ramonalopez@author7.com

bondagebyconcience@gmail.com

www.ramonalopez@forgivenessiskey.com